JOURNEY THROUGH SOUTH AFRICA

JOURNEY THROUGH
SOUTH AFRICA

GERALD CUBITT
& PETER JOYCE

C. STRUIK, CAPE TOWN

C. Struik (Pty) Ltd
Struik House, Oswald Pirow Street
Foreshore, Cape Town 8001

Reg. No. 80/02842/07

The following sources are acknowledged for black and white photographs
reproduced:
Africana Museum, Johannesburg: p9/8, 9, 11; p16/1, 4; p17/9, 13; p22/2,
    3, 5; p23/6.
Anglo American Corporation: p30/3.
Cape Archives: p8/1, 3; p9/6, 7; p16/3, 5; p17/8, 12; p23/7.
Cape Times: p37/10; p42/1, 4, 5; p43/6, 9.
Cape Times Collection, SA Library: p23/10; p30/1, 4, 5; p31/9, 10.
Die Burger: p23/11; p30/2, 6; p31/7, 8, 11; p36/1, 2, 3, 4, 5; p37/6, 7, 8,
    9; p42/2, 3; p43/7, 8, 10.
The Graphic: p16/6.
L. Hughes Collection, Johannesburg: p17/11.
Illustrated London News: p8/5.
Killie Campbell Collection, Durban: p8/4.
Local History Museum, Durban: p9/10.
Wilson, H.W., *After Pretoria*: p16/2; p17/10.

First published 1986

Designed by: Walther Votteler
Cover design by: Abdul Amien
Edited by: Phillida Brooke Simons
Reproduction by: Unifoto (Pty) Ltd, Cape Town
Typeset by: McManus Bros (Pty) Ltd, Cape Town
Printed and bound by: CTP Book Printers, Parow

ISBN 0 86977 274 0

BD5015

THE LAND AND ITS PEOPLE

South Africa is a big country; five times the size of Britain, about as large as Holland, Belgium, Italy, France and West Germany put together. It stretches from the Limpopo River in the north to blustery Cape Agulhas, nearly 2 000 kilometres to the south, from Namaqualand along the barren western seaboard 1 500 kilometres to subtropical Natal and the humid Indian Ocean coast: a total land area of 1 123 226 square kilometres.

This figure doesn't include the ten national states that lie within the Republic's borders. Four of them – Transkei, Bophuthatswana, Venda and Ciskei – are fully independent, though this autonomy is not accepted by the world at large. Also enclosed by South Africa are the separate kingdoms of Lesotho and Swaziland, both enjoying full diplomatic recognition.

Farther up the Atlantic coastline, beyond the desolate reaches of the Orange River, is Namibia, a vast and beautiful country of diamonds, desert and human division, that the League of Nations mandated to South Africa after the First World War. Flanking the Republic's far northern regions are, in clockwise order, the independent black states of Botswana, Zimbabwe and Mozambique. A rich territorial diversity.

Indeed, diversity is probably the single word that best illustrates both South and southern Africa. The canvas is kaleidoscopic; variety, contrast and sometimes conflict are vividly evident in the bewildering mix of race and language, creed, colour and culture. The diversity is there, too, in the nature of the land, in its geological formations and regional climates; its mountains, plains and coasts; its rich farmlands, its bushveld scrub and arid deserts, each of the many different parts supporting its own, distinctive plant and animal life. Truly, a world in one country.

PLATEAU AND PLAIN

In physical terms a significant portion of the land is very old. The subcontinent comprises 22 physiographic regions – different geological areas. Some of the rock strata in the valley of the Limpopo and in the northern Transvaal were formed 4 000 million years ago: not all that long, on the geological calendar, after planet earth itself began to cool. Others, those belonging to the Kalahari Group, are a mere two million years old. In between is a score of classifications that, together, tell a large part of the earth's story.

This variety accounts for South Africa's broad-based wealth of mineral resources. The ancient Swazian and Rondian formations, for instance, include gold-bearing reefs that, since their discovery just a hundred years ago, have transformed Transvaal's quietly rural Witwatersrand Highveld into a giant conurbation, recognized for the past half century and more as one of the world's mining and financial capitals. More recently gold, extensive reserves of it, was located in the Orange Free State. Also in the Transvaal, and farther to the west, there are rich iron and manganese deposits. Platinum and chrome are found in the central Transvaal; coal in the Karoo Sequence; diamonds in the Kimberlite pipes of the northern Cape; copper, zinc, uranium, cobalt, nickel – the list, 59 commodities in total, extends through almost the entire spectrum of metals and minerals. The only major ingredient missing is oil, and even reserves of that, in as yet undetermined quantities, have been charted off the southern shores.

The lie of the land. If you were to look down on South Africa from an orbiting satellite you would see a clear, quite simple topographical pattern. The land falls into two distinct physical regions: the great interior plateau, semicircular and occupying most of the subcontinent; and the 'marginal zone' which is the relatively narrow coastal and hinterland strip fringing the plateau on three sides. A third, strikingly obvious geographical feature is the division between the two regions: the highly (in the most literal sense) conspicuous and continuous necklace of mountains and hills known as the Great Escarpment.

The plateau is actually the southern tip of the Great African Plateau that rises in the Sahara Desert, some 5 000 kilometres to the north. In southern Africa its altitude varies from the comparatively low 600 metres of the Kalahari basin to an impressive 3 400 metres in the mountains of Lesotho.

Its subdivisions comprise, first, the basins: the bushveld north of the Transvaal uplands and of Bushmanland, and the upper Karoo – the lowest and driest parts of the plateau and known collectively as the 'middleveld'. Second, the plateau proper; vast, gently undulating plains studded with scatters of rocky outcrops and ridges (the classic Highveld, which Pretoria graces and over which Johannesburg and its urban satellites sprawl) and, in four of its subdivisions, rising to the upland 'blocks' of the Lesotho plateau to the east (the highest); the western heights that look over the southern Kalahari, and the northern ranges: the Waterberg and the Soutpansberg that roll down towards the Limpopo River.

The plateau's rim, the Great Escarpment, begins in the northeast with the craggy Transvaal Drakensberg (highest peak Mount Anderson 2 316 metres), then runs southwards, rising in even more splendid grandeur to the famed Natal Drakensberg's towering faces, some dropping near-vertically 2 000 metres to the plains below. Here are Mont-aux-Sources (3 282 metres); Champagne Castle (3 376 metres); Giant's Castle (3 314 metres); charming and evocative names for some of the most awesome peaks in the southern hemisphere. So formidable is the range that one 250 kilometre stretch may be traversed by just a single, steep route – the Sani Pass.

Southward still, the escarpment loops inland in a series of smaller ranges; the Stormberg of Anglo-Boer War fame; the Suurberg; the Sneeuberg north of the gracious little eastern Cape town of Graaff-Reinet. It then disappears into flatland for a while – through this thrust the major surface communications routes between Cape Town and the north – then rises in the granite formations of the Roggeveld Scarp and the Kamiesberg range (1 707 metres) and into Namaqualand.

Three hundred million years ago, when the single great land mass called Pangaea first began to succumb to continental drift, slowly, over hundreds of millennia, breaking up to create the global land patterns we know today, the stretch and pull of the earth's crust fashioned the most striking portion of South Africa's marginal zone – the Cape Folded Mountains. Legacies of the same mountain-building process are sister ranges in the Argentine and in Antarctica.

The series of Cape mountains, running parallel to each other and rising starkly over wide longitudinal valleys, include the Olifants River, Drakenstein, Hottentots Holland and the splendid Cedarberg (highest point: the 2 077 metre Great Winterhoek north of Tulbagh) ranges in the western parts, and the more intensively folded hills of Langeberg, Outeniqua, Tsitsikamma and Swartberg in the east, an area that also contains the Little Karoo basin, 30 by 60 kilometres in extent.

A much larger basin, the wide, shallow, world-famed Great Karoo, extends from the folded belts of the south and west northwards. Generally flattish but spliced by dramatic gorges, the most spectacular of which is probably the aptly named Valley of Desolation, it is an arid region: 'karoo' is derived from the Hottentot word meaning dry or bare. But still, there is the occasional small farming village, scattered flocks of sheep and lonely homesteads in this big, strangely beautiful land.

Water in a dry land. Only a small part of South Africa is blessed by good and regular rains (see page 7). Just a quarter of the country is nurtured by perennial rivers – they flow in the southern and south-western Cape and the eastern segment of the plateau. There are no real lakes – the large expanse of water called Fundudzi, in the northern Transvaal, was born of a massive landslide; the tourist-frequented 'lakes' of Zululand and the Knysna district of the Cape are in reality lagoons. So even the flow of the perennial streams and rivers depends on seasonal and, latterly, erratic rains. As for the great spaces of the western interior, their riverbeds fill and flow only after the rare summer storms. In South Africa, water is a precious commodity.

Biggest of the river systems is that of the Orange, running westwards from its headwaters in the high Natal Drakensberg for 2 250 kilometres to the Atlantic, plunging magnificently into the granite Augrabies gorge close to the Namibian border (in exceptional seasons the flow is greater than that of the better known Victoria Falls on the Zambezi River far to the north) before embarking on its last, desolate leg to the sea. Its tributaries include the Caledon and the Vaal, which is actually longer than its big brother but less voluminous.

The Orange drains almost the entire plateau – 47 per cent of the country. The eastern slopes of the plateau, on the other hand, are comparatively well-watered by their small rivers (one of the more substantial is the Letaba, well-known to game viewers in the Kruger National Park). They drain just 12 per cent of the country's surface area but contribute 40 per cent of the run-off. Of the other rivers of the plateau, Kipling's 'great grey-green, greasy Limpopo' is the most renowned, demarcating South Africa's northern frontiers with Botswana and Zimbabwe, gathering volume and momentum as it makes its way eastwards to the Indian Ocean north of the Mozambique capital of Maputo. Despite its legend in literature, however, it is not a major river by African standards.

Significant rivers of the marginal zone include the Sundays and Great Fish, both of which were crucial lines in the often violent territorial disputes between white settler and black tribesman in the nineteenth century (see page 24); the beautiful Berg River of the western Cape; and Natal's Tugela, where some of the most savage and, for the British, unrewarding battles of the Anglo-Boer War were fought. The Tugela, like the Orange, which flows in the opposite direction, rises at Mont-aux-Sources in the Drakensberg,

tumbles 600 metres down the Escarpment and then on, through 250 kilometres of attractive countryside to the eastern seaboard north of Durban. In volume it is larger than the better-known Vaal River, but it has a smaller drainage basin.

All told, though, South Africa's rivers do not amount to very much in world terms. Put together, their total run-off is equivalent to that of the Rhine at Rotterdam, and to just half that of the mighty Zambezi 1 000 kilometres to the north and about the same as the Mississippi in the United States.

Supplementary to the river systems are hundreds of pans, or 'floors' – shallow stretches of sometimes salty water (the result of evaporation), biggest of which is the 40 by 64 kilometre Groot Vloer in the north-western Cape. But the country's resources remain limited and precious: much of the modest volume is lost through spillage and through evaporation in the intense heat, and there is an ever-increasing demand from the farms, the cities and from industry. Consequently a number of ambitious hydro-engineering projects have been launched, some completed. Among them is the Orange River scheme, which accumulates an annual 7 500 million cubic metres of water, irrigates 300 000 hectares of farmland and provides an extra 2 200 million cubic metres for urban use. Its infrastructure includes the huge Hendrik Verwoerd and P.K. le Roux dams and a system of underground waterways, one of which is 82,5 kilometres long – the largest continuous water tunnel in the world. It irrigates the Great Fish River Valley to the south.

Vegetation. With the settlement of South Africa by black people from the north and by white colonists who created an enclave at the Cape in the 1650s and then spread steadily eastwards and northwards (see Part Two), much of the land was denuded of its natural vegetation, the cover either destroyed or replaced by exotic species. Nevertheless, five major groups, or vegetation communities, are clearly distinguished. They are those of:

☐ *The deserts and semi-deserts.* Excluding the huge and desolate expanses of the Namib, which are not within the Republic's borders, two areas fall into these categories. South Africa's only true desert region lies along the westward strip of Namaqualand extending into the lower Orange River Valley, a parched region that averages – depending on the precise locality – a scanty 50 to 150 millimetres of rainfall a year. In some years there is no rainfall at all. Vegetation is appropriately meagre: a thin ground cover of low, hardy, widely spaced shrubs and succulents and, in springtime, a blaze of bright desert annuals.

One notch higher on the vegetation scale is the Great Karoo, an enormous area of semi-desert with an uncertain rainfall averaging between 125 and 375 millimetres a year. Again, plant life comprises sparse, tough shrubs and succulents, though grasses occur – and sustain sheep where the veld is properly managed – in the more tolerable eastern regions.

☐ *The Mediterranean* (winter rainfall) areas of the south-western and southern Cape. Because of the immense wealth of its plant life, and despite its tiny area, this botanical region is regarded as one of the six floral kingdoms of the world. Forests are to be found only in the wetter kloofs, but many evergreen shrubs of various heights occur in this region as well as a vast number of indigenous species known collectively as *fynbos*. This includes the Cape's famed proteas (the king protea is South Africa's national flower), ericas and a marvellous diversity of bulbs. Characteristically, the plants here occur in small, localized areas and are therefore rather rare. They are believed to have ancient origins, and have been enabled to survive only because the Cape has escaped glaciation for millions of years.

☐ *The bushveld* covering the lower slopes of the plateau and the

Lowveld of the eastern Transvaal, an area that encompasses the great expanse of the Kruger National Park. Flora in the northern parts include marula and umbrella thorn, the elephantine baobab, the fever tree, the ubiquitous dark-green mopani and tall tufted grasses. In the more open Kalahari thornbush country, mainly towards the west, there are hardy acacia and camel-thorn trees and sparse semi-desert ground cover.

□ *The temperate interior uplands.* This is the classical veld consisting of rolling grassy plains and, probably because of winter droughts and frost, few trees (although some exotic species such as willows and eucalyptus – gum trees — thrive). Tropical-type grasses grow in the lower areas; in the colder upper parts, in the Highveld, the grass is shorter and indigenous trees are a rarity.

□ *The scattered forests* of the year-round rainfall belt, once widespread but victim to the depredations of man over the centuries. The relics of the marginal zone's great woodlands are now protected by law. Most extensive is the strip, 180 by 16 kilometres, along the southern coast where tall ironwood, yellowwood and stinkwood trees occur. Farther to the north, along the Natal coast, there are patches of evergreen subtropical tree species, including palms and, in the swampier areas, mangroves.

SEAS AND SHORES

Lapped by two oceans, South Africa's coastline runs 3 000 kilometres from the Atlantic wilderness of the Orange River mouth in the north-west, round the often stormy Cape to northern Natal and the Mozambique border in the east. Large stretches reward the traveller with spectacular scenery; some are a paradise for the angler, the surfer, the camper and the sun-worshipper.

Broadly speaking, the oceans fall into two type-categories: warm and cooler, the nature of each determined largely by the dominant currents of the subcontinental seas. The warm waters on the east coast of South Africa emanate from the tropics and flow rapidly south and south-west as the Agulhas Current, which more or less hugs the coast until, near Cape Agulhas, it turns south and east.

Along the west coast, the main waterbody comes from the South Atlantic as the north-flowing Benguela Current, and is much cooler. West of Cape Point and to the north, wind characteristics play a major role in determining water temperatures – strong offshore winds of the summer months cause coastal upwelling of cold water (as low as 7 °C) from the subsurface north-flowing Benguela Current; onshore or light winds reverse this process and are dominant in winter, when the average temperature is about 14,5 °C. Thus, because of the configuration of the coast in the vicinity of the Cape Peninsula and of the prevailing wind-patterns, the summer water temperatures between False Bay, open only on its south side, and Table Bay can differ by as much as 10 °C or 12 °C. Indeed, the Cape Peninsula is full of contrasts: apart from the 'two-oceans' syndrome, the monolithic presence of Table Mountain has a profound effect upon local weather conditions: the suburb of Newlands has a much higher rainfall than Sea Point; Clifton's sea can be glass-calm while a force four gale blusters over the waters off Milnerton.

The west coast is a strange, barren region of rocky, sand-blown shorelines backed by raised beaches and, stretching inland for anything between 30 and 50 kilometres, terraces of deep, soft, often-shifting sand. Dunes are covered by sparse greenery (technically, dwarf bush vegetation), and the land is classed as 'sandveld'. In the far north, around the mouth of the Orange, the legendary raised beaches are rich with diamonds, swept down by the river over the ages and then distributed by inshore currents.

The country's dynamic fishing industry has its home along the length of the west coast. Here, during the upwelling of the Atlantic — usually in spring and summer — rich plant nutrients are carried to the inshore zone, thus favouring the proliferation of plankton, basic to the area's rich stocks of mussels. These shellfish are primary feeders, and in their turn they support massive populations of rock lobsters, snoek and stockfish (Cape hake); in the south the sea at times abounds with tunny, marlin and yellowtail.

The south and east coasts are much more heavily populated and, in tourist terms, more popular. In the south, one stretch of shoreline with its hinterland is especially beautiful: the 220-kilometre Garden Route that extends roughly from Mossel Bay in the west to the Tsitsikamma Forest and Storms River in the east. This is a green and flowered region of charming bays and beaches, cliffs and pounding surf overlooked by the not-too-distant and quite splendid Outeniqua Mountains.

Equally enticing to holiday-makers are the coasts north and south of Durban in the east: wide, dune-backed sandy strips fringing a remarkably straight shoreline (Durban itself, with its 16 kilometre-long Bluff, is something of an exception).

In fact, there are precious few good natural harbours along the entire length of the Republic's coastline. (Saldanha Bay is the best, but it was passed over by the early seafarers in favour of the more exposed but better watered Table Bay.) It is an even coastline, without many pronounced embayments, and most of the otherwise-suitable estuaries are inhibited by sandbars, the product of currents and of the heavy sediment brought by rivers with steep gradients and sporadic flow. East London, in the far eastern Cape, is the country's only river port and its harbour, on the Buffalo, is subject to constant dredging operations. Durban's bar is particularly notorious. The city's port is one of the southern hemisphere's biggest and busiest, but it was only in 1892, after decades of frustrating experiment with breakwaters and sand-pumps, that the 2 820-ton *Dunrobin Castle* managed to sail into harbour – the first ocean-going liner to do so.

CLIMATE

Weather patterns, influenced by different ocean currents, by altitude and prevailing winds and by the ever-changing nature of the land, are subject to sharp regional variation. Climatically, South Africa could be half a dozen entirely separate countries.

When it comes to rainfall, however, there are three broad but distinct regions. The south-western tip of the subcontinent, centring round the lovely city of Cape Town, has winter precipitation; the southern and eastern coastal belts enjoy (in good years) perennial showers which are heavy, almost tropical in Natal. Rains over the rest of the country – on the great central plateau and towards the east – come with sudden summer thunderstorms brought by north-easterly winds.

This is not to say that the land, as a whole, is well-watered. On the contrary, South Africa is one of the world's drier countries: mean annual rainfall is little over 460 millimetres compared with a global average of 857 millimetres. The rains, too, tend to be unpredictable; drought has been the norm rather than the exception in recent times. And the farther west one goes the less generous the heavens are: along the shores of the Indian Ocean and in the Natal hinterland a healthy 1 000 millimetres of rain can be expected to fall each year; in the western extremities of the country the average tends to be around 200 millimetres, and some of the thirstlands are lucky if they get 50 millimetres.

Average annual temperatures are more constant. The northern areas are not, as one might perhaps expect, very much hotter than

SETTLEMENT AND CONQUEST. During the late fifteenth and in the sixteenth century Portuguese navigators, in the service of God and for the commercial profit of their royal patrons, charted the wind-blown shores of southern Africa, rounded the Cape and established sea-lanes to the spice-rich islands of the Indies. But the first permanent white settlement at the southern tip of Africa was Dutch, the seminal event the landing of Jan van Riebeeck and his small party of East India Company employees in April 1652. The Dutch ruled for 150 years before finally relinquishing control to Britain in 1806. In this time, they pushed their frontiers northwards and eastwards where they came into contact, and often bloody conflict, with the Nguni people. British solutions to the border

troubles included large-scale immigration schemes; the Boer reaction to an alien administration and to debilitating warfare against the Xhosa was to trek – to Natal and, more importantly, north across the Orange and Vaal rivers and into the domains of black chieftains, most powerful of whom was the redoubtable Mzilikazi. Meanwhile, the British were busy colonizing the eastern seaboard. By the late 1870s they had established their authority over the Zulu nation and, with the help of indentured Indian labour, were farming the lush land of Natal.

A Portuguese expedition plants a *padrão* – a stone cross – on the west coast (1). Van Riebeeck's arrival in Table Bay (2). The Bushmen (3) were the subcontinent's dominant race before being swept into near-oblivion, first by successive migrations of Bantu-speaking peoples and then by the relentless encroachments of white men. Skilled and hardy Huguenot refugees (4) joined the small Dutch community in 1688. British troops at the Cape, 1814 (5). The landing of the first British settlers in the eastern Cape, 1820 (6). Lord Charles Somerset (7), architect of the Cape's 'anglicization' programme. The Voortrekkers hold off Mzilikazi's impis at the Battle of Vechtkop, 1836 (8). British and Xhosa do battle during the War of the Axe (9), the seventh of nine frontier wars fought between 1779 and 1878. The Zulu king Shaka grants land around Port Natal to Lieutenant Farewell and his small band of British traders, 1824 (10). Indentured Indian labourers landing at Durban (11).

the southern because the land rises to the high central plateau, which is generally cooler than other parts of the world lying within the same lines of latitude. Cape Town can be suffocating and its annual average temperature is 17 °C; Pretoria, a full 1 500 kilometres nearer the tropics, can freeze and its annual average is only half a degree more. But again, air temperatures in the east are generally higher than those in the western coastal regions, affected respectively by the warm Agulhas and the cold Benguela currents. Temperature inversions also vary, quite dramatically, from place to place. They are least at the coast and greatest in the interior, where clear-skied winter nights are bitterly cold while the days remain sunny and mild.

South Africa, in fact, is blessed with a great deal of sunshine, the average number of cloud-free hours a day varying (depending on the area) from 7,5 to 9,4 compared with New York's 6,9, Rome's 6,4 and London's 3,8. Some parts of the country, the dust-dry western districts for instance, register a bare ten or so overcast days a year.

The climate of the interior, in the rising lands beyond the Escarpment, is fairly uniform: bone-dry, sunny winters; summer days (from about November to February) of mounting storm clouds and late-afternoon downpours. At least, that is the traditional pattern in the north-central and eastern parts, where, apart from Kimberley in the northern Cape, the inland cities and most of the towns are situated.

The climates of the different seaboard regions are more variable and interesting. The western Cape – Cape Town, the Peninsula, its coastal extensions and hinterland – is unique within the southern African context in its Mediterranean character. It has dry summers with long, cloudless days which are sometimes – in what are called 'berg wind conditions' (hot air blowing in from the northern interior) – perfect in their somnolent stillness, at other times disturbed by a gusty, unnerving south-easter that often reaches gale-force and can last for up to a week or more. In winter it is wet and cool – downright cold at times (snow falls on the surrounding mountains). The best Cape months are those of its brief spring (September and October) and autumn (March and April) when colours are changing and the fragile delicacy of the air lifts and sustains the spirit.

Northwards, up the Namaqualand coastal districts, the climate becomes ever drier and hotter until you eventually get to the Skeleton Coast and the endless, waterless tracts of the Namib Desert. Springtime in Namaqualand, though, is a lotion for the eyes: for a few brief weeks the barren desert countryside is transformed by multicoloured carpets of small, exquisite flowers.

Along the other coast, stretching east to Port Elizabeth, the climate changes from Mediterranean to temperate. Again the summers are warm (and windy); the winters cool. Here there is rainfall all year round – or there should be: the eastern Cape, like most of the rest of the country, has at times suffered crippling droughts. Following the Indian Ocean coastline as it inclines northwards, one enters the subtropical regions of Transkei and Natal, where it is hot and stickily humid in summer (though the uplands are cooler and very pleasant); chilly to warm in winter; and rainy throughout, but wetter during the summer months.

THE PEOPLE

South Africa, together with the independent national states (*see* page 14) had a total population of about 33 million in 1986 – one cannot be more exact because although censuses are taken periodically they are soon outdated, and the very nature of the society and the mobility of some of its elements make it difficult, if not impossible, to paint a precise statistical picture.

Of the four major ethnic groups, black people number some 28 million; whites nearly five million, those of Asian origin just under a million and the mixed-descent (coloured) community just under three million.

Growth rates vary quite sharply among groups – predictably, since South Africa is anything but homogenous. Most blacks have their roots in the countryside. They are of peasant farming stock, their traditional communities tribally structured. Cultural taboos and perceived economic necessity inhibit family planning; the extended family is an accepted and effective form of social security. Southern Africa is no different to the rest of the world: the poorer, less educated tend to have large families. With greater urbanization and higher standards of living a decline in the birth rate can be expected. At present, the black population is increasing by 2,7 per cent a year, which projects a total of something close to 40 million by the end of the century. By contrast, the annual white growth rate is 1,5 per cent, indicating (if one discounts the migration factor) a figure of about 5,5 million in the year 2 000. The mixed-descent community's yearly rate of increase is two per cent; the Asian 2,4 per cent.

The richness of the land and of what lies beneath it have dictated the concentrations of population. There are relatively high densities along the southern and eastern seaboards and in the Natal interior, in the central, northern and north-eastern Transvaal and the central Orange Free State.

A crucial feature of the past few decades has been urban drift, the migration both of whites and, more importantly, of blacks from the countryside to the cities. Until recently patterns were complicated by the Government's policy of influx control – the 'pass laws' have been abolished and the trend remains remorselessly steady. Industrial expansion since the Second World War has meant jobs, or at least the prospect of jobs, in and around the major centres, an irresistible lure to hundreds of thousands of blacks who would otherwise have to scratch a meagre living from the soil in areas that are not favoured by many modern amenities, and where, because of drought and overstocking and erosion, much of the land is poor and becoming even poorer. Biggest of the conurbations is the Pretoria-Witwatersrand-Vaal Triangle complex, South Africa's industrial heartland (*see* page 15). This immense cluster of concrete nuclei, each ringed by its dormitory suburbs, has a population of some six million: it covers less than one per cent of the country's land area but is home to almost a fifth of its people. Soweto – acronym for South-Western Townships – started life as a collection of 'locations' housing temporary labour for Johannesburg's giant gold mines. It is now a city in its own right, one of a million souls (that is the official figure – in reality it almost certainly accommodates a great many more), and its commuters include highly qualified people – artisans, executives, professional men – as well as miners and labourers.

Other centres – Cape Town, Port Elizabeth, Durban-Pinetown – have grown in similar fashion if rather less spectacularly. One source estimates that the ten million urban blacks in South Africa are expected to increase to at least 57 million by the year 2050, posing 'one of the major population problems of the next century'. Certainly, mass-migration to the cities will not be trouble-free, but urban drift is now regarded, in a number of authoritative quarters, not so much a problem as a natural, unstoppable process that could in fact help short-circuit, or at least alleviate, some of the country's most worrying anticipated ailments: badly needed infrastructural, social and other services, for instance, can be more easily and cheaply created for large concentrations of people than for widely scattered rural populations. Such endeavours as decentralization and influx control have proved enormously costly in terms of money, social relations and human dignity and probably cannot succeed. To allow freedom of movement will indeed lead to the creation of huge urban communities, but it is easier to provide people with jobs, with houses and clinics and schools, electric lighting, proper sanitation and all the other ingredients of a decent life if they are close to and part of the established centres. Moreover, quite apart from their potential as reservoirs of manpower, technical skills and professional expertise, large urban concentrations have a habit of becoming economically self-generative – much to their own and everybody else's benefit. This is the way many of South Africa's decision-makers are thinking in the 1980s, and the trend indicates a radical and healthy departure from the assumptions of the past.

At some time in the future it will probably be possible to write about the people of South Africa without too much qualification along racial lines, but today's reality is that the ethnic groups do not share a common heritage and are not, for reasons of law and in some cases of choice, integrated. Any objective summary must therefore take account of the separate identities.

The black people. Again, though somewhat less so (there are historical affinities), the blacks of southern Africa are divided by custom, social system and language into a number of groupings. The divisions are not clearly evident in the party-political arena nor in the context of increasingly detribalized urban life, but in other respects the principal black groups can be regarded as distinctive societies. They comprise the Zulu, the Xhosa, the Swazi (all three are related, belonging to the Nguni group of people); the Northern Sotho, the Southern Sotho and the Tswana (again, of the same major Sotho group: the Tswana are the western branch); the South Ndebele and the North Ndebele; the Venda and Lemba; and the Shangaan-Tsonga. To elaborate a little:
☐ The two biggest components of the northern Nguni are the Swazi, now largely settled in the independent kingdom of Swaziland in the north-eastern part of the subcontinent (although KaNgwane, a self-governing national state within South Africa, is home to hundreds of thousands of their kinsmen); and the Zulu, a name now given to the many subgroups of the Nguni people who were forged into a single, powerfully coherent society by the great nineteenth century leader Shaka.

The Zulu 'homeland' is KwaZulu, adjoining Natal and led by Chief Mangosuthu Buthelezi. His six million people form the largest of southern Africa's ethnic blocks, and are entitled to fully independent (republican) status within Pretoria's formal policy of separate development, but decline to take up the option. The pragmatic Buthelezi regards himself as a South African; advocates a unitary state in which power is shared rather than split; concedes that such a system will take time and a great deal of hard-headed negotiation to achieve; and in the interim appears willing to settle for, among other things, a joint democratic venture with the whites and Asians of Natal.
☐ The southern Nguni comprise a number of sub-groups, most numerous being the Pondo, Tembu and, especially, the Xhosa, with whom the white settlers of the Cape came into bloody contact in the eighteenth and nineteenth centuries, waging nine full-scale frontier wars (*see page 24*). These Nguni populate the independent republics of Transkei and Ciskei, fairly recently carved out of the eastern Cape Province.
☐ The Ndebele people in the north are related to the Matabele of Zimbabwe, who are of Nguni origin – their founder, Mzilikazi, rebelled against Shaka and, at the conclusion of a blood-soaked odyssey, led his followers north of the Limpopo in 1838. The Ndebele of the Transvaal, many of whom are settled in the self-governing state of KwaNdebele, are in turn divided into the southern section, which retains its Nguni heritage, and the northern,

which has relinquished the Nguni identity and language and is now culturally part of the Sotho peoples which, to confuse matters even further, also fall into three separate though related groups:
☐ The Northern Sotho, of whom the Pedi are the largest segment, make up the population of the national state of Lebowa; the Southern Sotho inhabit both the independent and internationally recognized state of Lesotho and the South African-sponsored national state of Qwaqwa; and thirdly, the Tswana, citizens of the independent but not generally recognized Republic of Bophuthatswana, a scatter of territories with a capital, Mmabatho, a popular television station and – one of its major sources of revenue – the glittering tourist mecca of Sun City. Other Tswana groups form part of the population of the neighbouring state of Botswana.
☐ The Venda, too, have their own national state, a tiny segment of real estate bordering the northern Transvaal close to the Kruger National Park. Venda's population numbers some 400 000, which include the still-distinctive but increasingly assimilated Lemba people.
☐ Finally, the Shangaan-Tsonga, something over a million strong, are neighbours of the Venda and Northern Sotho. The Shangana people in fact straddle the South African-Mozambique border, though they have been granted a home state, Gazankulu, in the northern Transvaal.

All this might suggest that South Africa's black communities have clung tenaciously to traditional African ways and remain outside the mainstream of western influence, which of course is patently not so. Custom, tradition and ancient loyalties do persist, most obviously but not exclusively in the rural areas. They are enshrined, for instance, in the rules of courtship and marriage (usually those sanctioning polygamy); in matters of inheritance and guardianship, and seniority within the clan; in kinship bonds, the social order and the spiritual force of ancestry; and in the assumptions underlying land tenure and in concepts of wealth.

That is the old Africa. The new co-exists (often uncomfortably) and will in due course supersede. Many of the ten million urban blacks are second and third generation townsmen; hundreds of thousands are migrant workers; all have been dramatically exposed to the blessings and curses of the acquisitive society. The tribal order, in the towns, has been largely eroded, to be replaced by a transitional but distinct subculture that encompasses (engulfs, in many tragic instances) everything from social structure and family life to music, literature and language.

Whether urbanization and its multiple assault on African tradition is a good or a bad thing, is a complex issue, the conclusion subjective. What is no longer open to question, though, is the inevitability of the process. South Africa is an industrial nation, increasingly dependent on the skills of black people to keep the production lines moving. The blacks for their part are impelled to go – and to live – where there is work. And so the sprawl of the cities continues, shifting the economic balance. In the years 1973 to 1977 – by no means a boom period – the real earnings of blacks rose an impressive annual six per cent; those for whites actually dropped a percentage point. By 1978 the combined earnings of blacks made up 40 per cent of the national wage bill. Three years later the Bureau of Economic Research at Stellenbosch University disclosed that the average black family's income – outside the agricultural sector – was R2 736 a year, still far short of white earnings but the wage gap was closing rapidly. In the giant mining industry the white/black earnings ratio was 19,79:1 in 1970, narrowing to 7,57:1 in 1977. Average black incomes have been rising dramatically in real terms since then, their total now on about parity with – and will soon enough overtake – white earnings;

black spending power is also about half the total and will by the end of the century expand to twice the amount spent in the entire consumer market of the mid-1980s.

One can go on citing figures, but the picture is clear enough. Black South Africans, especially those of the swelling city communities, command a great deal of economic muscle, which they are able to demonstrate effectively through legitimate trade union negotiation and action (and, sporadically, through the less formal means of consumer boycott). Certainly, this has profound political implications.

In these circumstances, many of the convictions underlying government policy since the Verwoerdian era and before (see page 33) must be, and are being, brought into question. Millions of people firmly settled in and around the towns can no longer be regarded as 'temporary' visitors whose proper place is elsewhere, in a national state, and the issues of domicile, property ownership and citizenship are subject to wide-ranging debate and re-examination. At the time of going to press, abolition of influx control and the 'pass laws', in April 1986, are to date the heaviest broadsides fired during the continuing reformist offensive. They have been replaced by a policy of 'orderly urbanisation'.

The Asian people. A need for labour to harvest the crops of Natal's new and vast sugar plantations in the mid-nineteenth century prompted the importation of tens of thousands of workers from India. They were indentured (contracted) for between three and five years, after which they had the choices of repatriation, of renewing their contracts, or of accepting Crown land and remaining as settlers. Most took up the land option.

The first shipload disembarked in 1860. In due course they were joined by non-indentured 'passenger' immigrants from the Indian subcontinent – British subjects able to travel freely within the Empire, and choosing the sunbathed spaces of Natal as their future home. Today, South Africa's Asian community numbers some 900 000, most of whom – 85 per cent – live in and around the Durban-Pinetown complex. Nearly all the remainder, about 100 000 people of Asian origin, are settled on the Witwatersrand and in Pretoria. Among them are 10 000 or so citizens of Chinese extraction who retain their own cultural identity.

The Indian society, generally a prosperous one, has its own distinct traditions, underpinned by religion and by the *kutum* – the disciplined, patriarchal extended family which regulates relationships and social interaction. The community is remarkably unified but also organized according to faith – Hindu and Muslim. The Hindu element is in turn divided into four language groups (Tamil, Telugu, Hindustani and Gujarati) and subscribes to its own fairly strict rules governing modes, manners, ritual, food and drink. The Muslims speak Gujarati – the language of western India – and Urdu, and observe precisely defined codes of belief and behaviour.

Again, though, traditions are being eroded, especially among the younger generation. The izar and qami, the dawni and sari are giving way, if not always to T-shirts and jeans, certainly to the more conservative western styles of dress; there is movement away from the multiple towards the smaller family; traditional male authority no longer goes unquestioned; young Indian women lead far freer and more diversified lives than their mothers and grandmothers; and English is by and large the means of communication.

Always a significant component of the South African economy – the community has an exceptionally high proportion of professionals and entrepreneurs – the Indians were ushered into the body politic with the creation of the tricameral constitutional system in 1984 (see page 39) and now have some say in the conduct of national affairs.

South Africans of mixed descent. The country's nearly three million-strong coloured community, the majority of whom live in the western Cape, has diverse origins. The early Dutch settlers imported slaves from Holland's eastern possessions, from elsewhere in Africa and from some of the islands of the Atlantic and Indian oceans, and admixtures steadily and inevitably followed, Hottentot, Xhosa and white man adding their own progeny over the following decades.

Significant subgroups include the Griquas of the north-eastern and north-western Cape, the product of European-Hottentot miscegenation; the mixed-descent people of Natal, many of whom trace their ancestry to immigrants from Mauritius and St Helena; and the 200 000 Cape Malays of the Peninsula, a close-knit society that has maintained its strict Islamic ways over the centuries since their forebears arrived from Indonesia, Malagasy, Ceylon (now Sri Lanka) and China.

In general terms, though, the coloured people of South Africa are culturally very much part of the western world. Some 87 per cent are of the Christian faith; the majority speaks Afrikaans; and they are barely separable in lifestyle and social organization and aspiration from people of exclusively European origin. There seems no good reason why they should be subject to any special classification (not that formally imposed ethnic categories of any kind can be justified), and in fact were more or less an integrated part of the Cape community as a whole until fairly recently, enjoying, among other things, the constitutionally entrenched common-roll franchise, until it was removed in the 1950s. Coloured residential areas are delineated; the famed District Six, close to the heart of Cape Town, was demolished in the late 1970s and early 1980s and most of its inhabitants moved to the huge, new and somewhat characterless townships such as Mitchell's Plain on the Cape Flats. The move was not a popular one and the site of District Six remains largely undeveloped; a scar on Cape Town's landscape and on the minds of its citizens.

Nevertheless, the racial lines remain blurred; there is a degree of social and residential mixing – a degree that grows larger by the year – and of political advancement. In a manner of speaking, the vote was restored to the coloured people with the introduction of the tricameral parliamentary system in 1984.

The white people. South Africa has two official languages, Afrikaans and English, reflecting the dual origins of its politically dominant ethnic group.

The Afrikaners are descendants of the early Cape-Dutch settlers and of people of the other nationalities they absorbed, together numbering something over 2,5 million today. High Dutch was the stem from which the language branched, taking on new words and a different shape over three centuries of isolation from the original homeland and, later, from the principal Cape settlement.

The German and French elements are significant (and, linguistically, the black languages as well): the Afrikaners in fact have a rich mix of cultures in their blood, one official estimate pegging the ancestral ingredients at only 40 per cent Dutch, a surprising 40 per cent German; 7,5 per cent British (mainly Scots); 7,5 per cent French and five per cent others. The French connection, through the hardy Protestant Huguenots who fled persecution in Europe in the 1680s, can be discerned in names such as Du Plessis, Du Toit and Marais; the Dutch in the 'van' prefixes. Curiously, there seems to be very little that is clearly German in language, custom or nomenclature – assimilation seems to have been total.

Over the decades, the Afrikaner community expanded from very small beginnings, more as a consequence of natural increase than from immigration (hence the proliferation of certain names –

the confusing concentration of Bothas in Government, for instance). Families have always tended to be large, patriarchal, Calvinistic and close-knit; groups of families clannish – the universal characteristics of pioneer people.

Despite the mixture of antecedents, and despite bouts of bitter factionalism, the story of the Afrikaner has been one of fierce pride in nation, of unity under threat, and of tough and uncompromising cultural exclusivity. All of which is understandable enough: the early settlers, especially those of the eastern Cape, found plenty of lonely hardship in a land made inhospitable by the elements, natural hazard and the violence of man, and came to trust for survival in musket, Bible and the closing of ranks. Then, with the establishment of British rule, at the beginning of the nineteenth century, came greater bureaucratic control, a degree of deprivation and a threat to their identity. So in the 1830s they inspanned their ox-wagons and trekked into the great northern wilderness in search of peace, living-space and the right to live their own lives unmolested, none of which they found in lasting measure. Fabulous deposits of gold were located beneath the pastoral surface of their Promised Land; foreigners flocked into the fledgling Boer states and once again the Afrikaners felt themselves besieged, a fear that was brutally confirmed by the Jameson Raid of 1895-96 and the cynical diplomatic prelude to full-scale war three years later (see Part Two).

In short, from their early settler years, Afrikaners saw themselves as a hounded and beleaguered people – and with some justice. It was only towards the middle of the present century that Afrikanerdom – not the bridge-building kind of Louis Botha and Smuts but the Afrikanerdom of J.B.M. Hertzog, D.F. Malan and H.F. Verwoerd – could challenge English-speaking South Africans for economic and political dominance.

This, put briefly and perhaps simplistically, is the historical legacy. The heirs to it, in extremely broad terms, can be divided into two groups: conservatives, who think and act very much like their forebears; and those who see other realities and, in degrees varying from the cautious moderate to the intellectual-radical, want change and accommodation within a new social and political order.

South Africa is home to just under two million English-speaking whites, and their legacy is entirely different from that of the Afrikaners (though voting patterns indicate a substantial identity of interest between the two main linguistic groups). The background is colonial rather than pioneer; urban-industrial rather than rural.

There were half a dozen watershed events (which are covered in more detail in Part Two) in the history of the English-speaking settlement. First was the British occupation of the Cape (technically, two occupations: the first between 1795 and 1803, and the second from 1806 onwards) during the French Revolutionary and Napoleonic wars, when the landing of the redcoats ended over a century of Dutch East-India Company rule and ushered in an era of deliberate 'anglicization'. Part of this process was the second major influx: the arrival of 4 000 or so settlers at Algoa Bay in the eastern Cape in 1820. Farther east, the colonization of Natal – a more independently motivated exercise – gathered momentum from the 1840s with a series of privately organized immigration schemes.

The fourth, essentially two-pronged English onslaught, was the birth of South Africa's huge mining industry with the discovery of diamonds in the northern Cape (near present-day Kimberley) in 1867 and of gold on the Witwatersrand in 1886. These drew large numbers of 'Uitlanders' (outlanders, or aliens) to the northern areas, most of whom were English-speaking. Much later, further fairly large migrations occurred with mass-demobilization after the Second World War and, in the post-colonial era, with the

granting of independence to Britain's East African territories and Zambia, which produced a trickle of immigrants. Recent years have witnessed the slow, convulsive demise of unilaterally independent white Rhodesia (now Zimbabwe), which prompted something of a flood.

The strongholds of the present English-speaking community were thus historically determined. It is no accident that South Africa's English universities are at Cape Town (UCT), Grahamstown (Rhodes University), in Natal (Durban and Pietermaritzburg) and Johannesburg (The University of the Witwatersrand). Other than significant English-speaking farming communities in the eastern Cape and in the sugar and fruit-growing regions of Natal, it is very largely an urban community.

Traces of the colonial psychology persisted until well after the Second World War. In affluent homes along the gracious tree-lined avenues of Constantia in the Cape and in Pietermaritzburg people would speak, in accents indistinguishable from those of upper-middle-class Surrey and Sussex, of England as 'home', toast the Queen on her birthday and eat plum pudding in the mid-day heat of a southern Christmas. But these now represent very much of an anachronistic minority. Most English-speaking South Africans have long since detached themselves from their ancestral origins and identify wholly with the country, although some of their children, for a number of reasons unconnected with a sense of belonging, do tend to drift away, many of them to Britain.

Until fairly recently, too, the English-speaking section had virtual monopoly on the non-agrarian economy; the reins of commerce and industry were firmly in Anglo-Saxon and Jewish hands. This is no longer the case. Even before Afrikanerdom assumed control of central government and the bureaucracy in 1948 it was flexing its economic muscles. Today substantial segments of the private sector, notably vast insurance and financial conglomerates, are run by Afrikaans-speakers.

A number of smaller ethnic and linguistic groups make up the residue of the white community. Most substantial – estimates vary widely but there are probably about 75 000 – are South Africans of Portuguese extraction, most of them former residents of Lisbon's African territories of Mozambique and Angola, both now independent, though a substantial number hail from the Atlantic island of Madeira. In descending numerical order the additional groups are the German (40 000); Greek (17 000); Italian (17 000); and French (7 000). Together, other nationalities total some 35 000.

A significant subgroup of English-speaking South Africans are the Jewish people, comprising about 2,5 per cent of the white population. Though relatively small in numbers, Jewish South Africans have contributed markedly to the business and industrial development of the country: personalities of the past such as Barney Barnato, Lionel Phillips, Samuel Marks and Alfred and Otto Beit played prominent parts in the early days of the diamond- and gold-fields. In the world of the arts, both performing and visual and in literature, so many Jews have distinguished themselves that it would be invidious to single out any name. Among those Jews who have played significant rôles in politics the name of Helen Suzman is today among the most highly respected. Celebrated both in South Africa and internationally as industrialists and philanthropists are the late Sir Ernest Oppenheimer and his son Harry, though this family is no longer of the Jewish faith.

WHERE THE PEOPLE LIVE: TERRITORIES AND CITIES

The country is formally divided into four provinces and a number of black national states at varying stages of political autonomy.

In 1910 the Crown colonies of Natal and the Cape of Good

Hope and the former Boer republics of the Transvaal and the Orange Free State were brought together as provinces of the Union of South Africa (see page 28). Until 1986 the provincial authorities enjoyed a healthy degree of administrative and some legislative autonomy, but there are plans to replace them with a restructured multi-racial system of Regional Services Councils (see page 40).

Cheek-by-jowl are the black homelands, or national states, which have already been touched on (page 14). These will be mentioned from time to time throughout this narrative, and because the arrangement is complicated – downright confusing, perhaps, to the uninvolved observer – it would be as well to summarize the territorial units at this point. The four independent republics are:

□ *Transkei:* a once-fertile, beautiful country of 45 000 square kilometres on the eastern seaboard (its Wild Coast is famed) between the Kei and the Mtamvuna rivers. Population: approximately 3 000 000; capital: Umtata; Prime Minister: George Matanzima.

□ *Bophuthatswana:* a fragmentation of seven major territorial blocks totalling 40 000 square kilometres and situated within three of South Africa's provinces (Transvaal, Cape and Orange Free State). Population: approximately 1 700 000; capital: Mmabatho, close to the rail junction of Mafikeng, which Bophuthatswana absorbed during the consolidation process. Income from maize, beef, gambling (at the Sun City hotel and entertainment complex), and from the platinum group of metals, of which it is the world's third largest producer. Executive President: Chief Lucas Mangope.

□ *Ciskei:* an area of 9 000 square kilometres lying between the Great Fish River and the Border corridor along the Great Kei River. Population: approximately 900 000; capital: Bisho. Economic base is subsistence agriculture; income is generated by 40 000 workers who commute daily to East London and King William's Town, and by 50 000 migrant labourers working mainly on the Witwatersrand. Executive President: Chief Lennox Sebe.

□ *Venda:* 6 000 square kilometres in area (it is the smallest and poorest of the independent national states) situated in the northern Transvaal east of the Soutpansberg range, west of the Kruger National Park. The Limpopo is its northern border with Zimbabwe. Population: approximately 400 000; capital: Thohoyandou. The economy is based on subsistence agriculture; principal sources of income are its 50 000 migrant workers. Executive President: Patrick Mphephu.

In addition there are six self-governing states, which may or may not apply for full republican status at some future date. KwaZulu dwarfs the others: it comprises ten separate land units on the eastern seaboard and inland, totalling some three million hectares in area. KwaZulu's population is about 4 000 000; its gross national product is in excess of R2 000 million. Chief Minister is Mangosuthu Buthelezi. The other five self-governing states are Gazankulu (population: approximately 600 000); Lebowa (approximately 2 000 000); Qwaqwa (approximately 200 000); KaNgwane (approximately 400 000), and KwaNdebele (approximately 200 000).

The whole structure represents a massive exercise in human logistics. The Native Lands Act of 1913 and the Native Trust and Land Act of 1936 demarcated traditional black areas – just under 17 million hectares out of a total South African land area of 122 million hectares. The latter Act also gave the State the right to consolidate the patchwork and to remove people to their designated homelands. Such removals started in earnest around 1950, reaching a high plateau of activity between 1960 and 1980, during which years some 3,5 million blacks were relocated. The sus-

tained operation was controversial; the disruption monumental; and the cost, both in terms of human relations and finance, enormous. In 1985 President P.W. Botha's government announced a fundamental change of policy (see page 40) and, in the following year, gave dramatic substance to the promise: influx control and the pass laws disappeared from the statute books; forced removals ceased.

A glance at the above population figures makes it clear that a great many blacks, nominally citizens of one or another national or self-governing state, actually live in the Republic of South Africa. A great many, as mentioned (see page 11) have congregated in and around the urban complexes, principal of which, in order of age, are:

□ Cape Town, which had its beginnings in 1652 with the landing of Jan van Riebeeck and his small party of settlers. Greater Cape Town – the magisterial districts of the Cape, Goodwood, Kuils River, Wynberg and Simon's Town – sprawls over much of the Peninsula and is home to between 1,5 and two million people: about half a million whites, 800 000 citizens of mixed descent, and 200 000 blacks. The city's setting, beneath and around the moody grandeur of Table Mountain, is without doubt one of the loveliest in the southern hemisphere. Circumnavigator Francis Drake is credited with describing the region 'the fairest Cape in all the circumference of the earth'; later, as one of the busiest harbours on the long sea route to India, the town became known, rather more prosaically, as the 'tavern of the seas'.

Cape Town's port is quieter than it was in the heyday of the passenger steamer. And other harbours, much closer to the northern industrial markets, have poached much of its freight traffic. Marine and mercantile enterprises still contribute substantially to the local economy, though. Its wider base includes light engineering and manufacturing, the service industries (many large companies have their headquarters in Cape Town, mainly, it seems, because it is such a pleasant place in which to live) and tourism – the beaches, the attractive wineland-and-mountain hinterland, the history in the stones of the buildings, the calendar of arts, the eating and drinking places, and the undemanding, unhurried lifestyle are powerful attractions. A great many affluent people retire to or near the city. The Peninsula is 1 463 kilometres from Johannesburg, 1 716 kilometres from Durban, and its residents sometimes tend to feel left out of things.

□ It is difficult to say with certainty whether Port Elizabeth or Durban is South Africa's second-oldest city. Probably Port Elizabeth, which is where the 1820 Settlers set their optimistic feet ashore – or rather, on the beaches of Algoa Bay, since there was just a dilapidated fort and a tiny cluster of thatched cottages on the site of the city at that time. It is now a great port, but it took decades to grow into anything resembling such. As late as 1838 a visitor could write of 'an ugly, dirty, ill-built, ill-scented hamlet similar to some of the worst fishing villages on the English coast'. But the port did eventually develop (it formally became a city in 1913) into an impressive modern complex of dockyards, motor assembly plants, factories and commercial buildings sustaining, together with its satellites of Uitenhage and Kirkwood, some 300 000 economically active people. It has about 80 black schools, 60 white schools, 45 coloured and Asian schools, and a university. Not far away is Grahamstown, familiarly known as the 'city of the saints' because of its many churches. Overlooked by the impressive lecture and theatre complex of the 1820 British Settlers' Monument, home of Rhodes University and of several famous schools, Grahamstown, keeper of English South Africa's soul, is probably among the most attractive of the country's smaller centres.

□ Durban, on the Natal coast and third-largest of the cities is aptly known as 'South Africa's playground', though it is more reminiscent of Blackpool than of Cannes. Durban is not, however, the capital of Natal: that honour belongs to the pretty little city of Pietermaritzburg some 90 kilometres inland.

Durban's origins, and its history, are very English. It started life as the trading and white-hunter outpost of Port Natal when, in 1824, the enterprising Lieutenant Farewell of the good ship *Julia* (he had previously served on the *Beagle* of Darwinian fame) disembarked 40 white settlers, to whom the Zulu king Shaka, with surprising benevolence, granted 9 000 square kilometres of rich land around the bay. Progress was slow at first (in 1835 there were still only 30 or so residents), but with the launching of immigration schemes in the 1840s the town expanded rapidly. Today, more than a million and a half people inhabit the Durban-Pinetown complex; its 1 668-hectare bay area has 15 195 metres of quayside that handles bulk cargoes of, among other commodities, grain, coal, manganese, and sugar from the plantations. The local industrial and commercial base is broad, food-processing and, predictably, marine-orientated businesses such as warehousing and oil storage being prominent.

□ Bloemfontein, capital of the Orange Free State and judicial capital of the Republic of South Africa, sprawls over 16 900 hectares of dry, treeless central plateau countryside. The origin of its name has never been firmly established but the consensus seems to be that it was derived from 'Bloem', an adventurous and much-loved ox belonging to trekker Martinus Brits who built his homestead on the site of the present city in 1840. Legend has it that after the unfortunate Bloem had been devoured by a lion, his memory was perpetuated in the name of the farm and, in due course, in that of the town that grew up there, the land having been bought in 1848 (for £37.10s) as headquarters of the Orange River Sovereignty's Resident, Major H.D. Warden.

Bloemfontein, now the home of some 300 000 people, is largely an administrative city (though it has 350 or so light industries, and the largest railway workshops in the country) – 40 per cent of its economically active citizens are employed in social, community or government services. The town is quiet, serious, respectable. It has some fine buildings, notably the Raadsaal, or parliament – a dignified mix of Renaissance form and Classical-revival detail – and the splendid new Opera House, completed in 1985.

□ Pretoria, State administrative capital and a place of some one million souls, is known as the 'jacaranda city' because of the 50 000 or so lovely lilac-blossomed trees that grace gardens, parks and about 650 kilometres of well-laid-out streets. The city has a magnificent general setting, overlooked by hills on which the renowned architect Herbert Baker placed his Union Buildings, model for the grander but no more pleasing seat of the Raj government in New Delhi. There are other impressive structures, especially the turn-of-the-century Palace of Justice, described as 'one of the finest classical public spaces in South Africa'. Church Square has always been Pretoria's hub, but nowadays is not a very attractive one. At the time of Union it could have become one of the architectural glories of the subcontinent, embellished with fountains and flowers and Continental-style paving (this was the citizenry's preference). Instead, the civic authorities chose to redesign it as a tramway terminus. Says author Vivien Allen: 'Pretoria exchanged its heart for a public transport system.'

□ Sixty kilometres south of Pretoria is the financial and industrial epicentre of South Africa: the Witwatersrand, with the high-rise density of Johannesburg at its centre. In fact there is not much open country between Pretoria and Johannesburg, and there will be even less in the coming decade during which a brand new city will progressively cover much of the intervening dun-and-green veld. Its focal point is the aptly and charmingly named village of Halfway House but the planners, in their pedestrian fashion, have chosen to call the future metropolis Midrand.

The Witwatersrand has an inner and an outer ring of towns. The former, around metropolitan Johannesburg, comprises the largely dormitory municipalities of Sandton (rich, chic, and pretentious), Randburg, Roodepoort, Edenvale, Germiston, Alberton (the last two somewhat downmarket), Bedfordview and Soweto, the largest black urban complex in the country. The outer zone includes the substantial centres of Krugersdorp (Dr Jameson's Waterloo – *see* page 27), Randfontein, Westonaria, Kempton Park (which has a fine racetrack), Benoni, Springs and Boksburg. The official population is around four million; the real one almost certainly a great deal higher.

These towns are built on gold, discovered just a hundred years ago (*see* page 27), which still sustains them but not by any means exclusively – about 60 per cent of the entire country's gross product is generated by the huge number of mining, manufacturing, commercial and financial enterprises in the area.

Johannesburg itself has a population of between 1,5 and two million. Its buildings are tall, new and closely packed (the central flatland area of Hillbrow is the densest residential area in the southern hemisphere), and the whole seems to have been laid out by some lunatic town planner with a grudge against motorists.

Nobody can pretend Johannesburg is a beautiful city. It is notably lacking in open spaces; the mine-dumps are an eyesore (though most of them now have thin coats of greenery: an improvement on the dust-blown past). But there is a vibrancy, a bustling, honestly materialistic vitality about the place that does have its appeal. And it has a marvellous climate: it is situated high on the central plateau where the air is rare and heady, the winters clear and not too cold, the summer heat (in good years) relieved by late-afternoon rainstorms that are often cloudbursts of Lear-like proportions. On average Johannesburg gets more rain in little more than four summer months than England's notoriously soggy Manchester does in a full year.

BOER AGAINST BRITON. The discovery of diamonds in the northern Cape in the late 1860s and of massive deposits of gold on the Witwatersrand in 1886 fueled the engine of Imperial expansionism and threatened the independence of the two northern Boer republics. The result: two major wars, the second and more devastating triggered by, among other events, Dr Jameson's provocative raid into the Transvaal on New Year's Day, 1897.

This period also saw the last and greatest of the black backlashes against nineteenth century colonial conquest.

The Battle of Isandlwana in 1879 (1) where the large British force was virtually annihilated by Cetshwayo's Zulu army. Household Cavalry showing the flag (2) after the annexation of the Transvaal, an event which led directly to the Transvaal War of 1880-81 and another humiliating British defeat, this one on the bloody slopes of Majuba Hill (7).

The diamond-rich Big Hole at Kimberley, 1872 (3). Paul Kruger (4), patriarchal President of the South African Republic (the Transvaal), and (5) his arch-enemy in the corridors of southern African power, the ruthless visionary Cecil Rhodes. Hordes of prospectors — *uitlanders*, or foreigners — descended on the northern territories in the 1870s and 1880s (6).

The gulf between Briton and Boer became an unbridgeable chasm after the Jameson Raid, and the Anglo-Boer War erupted three years later. The relief of Boer-besieged Ladysmith, February 1900 (8). Boer hit-and-run tactics (9) succeeded in protracting hostilities for a further 18 exhausting months. Christiaan de Wet (11), was one of the most gifted of the guerilla leaders. British commander-in-chief Kitchener replied with scorched earth, barbed wire, blockhouse and concentration camp. Pictured are displaced Boer women *en route* to internment (10). Peace at last: Generals Louis Botha and Kitchener after the Treaty of Vereeniging (12).

THE PAST

Often in the telling, perhaps too often, South Africa's story begins with a tiny band of hardy seventeenth century Dutchmen making their landfall beneath the grandeur of Table Mountain, on the southern tip of the subcontinent, to create the first permanent white settlement on Francis Drake's 'fairest Cape'.

That was of course the first really significant landmark in the annals of the modern, structured state, but for millennia before southern Africa had been home to darker-skinned people. Archaeological finds indicate that the Bushmen, or Khoisan, began to drift southwards across the Zambezi fully 1 500 years ago; they were small bands of nomadic hunter-gatherers who roamed the great sunlit spaces in search of sustenance and solitude, a unique culture that once flourished but has now all but disappeared. For a protracted time, throughout the Later Stone Age, they were the dominant people in the vast area that stretched from today's Namibia eastwards to Natal and from the Limpopo to Agulhas on the stormy southern Cape coast.

Not that the word 'dominant', and all that it suggests, is appropriate in the context of Bushman society. Entirely without hostility, these gentle, extraordinary people had – still have – a profound belief in sharing: in co-operation within the family, between clan and clan, between man and his environment. Custom and conviction excluded personal antagonism; nature, both animate and inanimate, was sanctified, hallowed in the mystic rituals of the hunt and the trance-like dance, and in the lively cave-paintings and engravings that grace some 2 000 recorded sites throughout southern Africa.

Later on came other peoples, succeeding migratory waves that washed southwards to mingle with, sometimes to fight against and eventually displace, the Bushmen. One of the first were the Hottentots – the Khoikhoi, or 'men of men' as they called themselves – who, although related to the small-statured hunters of the plains, were pastoralists, herders of cattle living in fairly well organized tribal groupings and conscious of territorial rights. These were the people with whom the explorers and circumnavigators of Portugal and England, France and Holland first came into contact on the shores of the Cape, a meeting that usually resulted in mutually profitable barter but occasionally in deadly combat.

The Bantu-speaking people were comparative late-comers. Negroid-Hamitic groups from the tropical central African regions (with ancestral origins in the Nilotic north-east), they had engulfed much of the sub-Saharan continent by the time the first Cape Europeans started putting down their pioneering roots. By the fourteenth century they had occupied what is today Zimbabwe, eastern Botswana and the western parts of the Transvaal (although earlier Iron Age black men, of different cultures, had settled in parts of these areas centuries before).

Much of the story of black migration is shrouded in mystery, and theories are both numerous and complex. It is generally agreed, though, that four main groups were involved: the Sotho, the Nguni, the Tsonga and the Venda. By the late seventeenth century their spearhead, the Xhosa (of the southern Nguni group)

were stabbing into the eastern Cape, on a direct collision course with the expanding white farming communities. Inevitably, competition for living space would lead to bitter conflict.

Inevitably, too, the Bushman population would be depleted almost to the point of extinction through the encroachment of better organized, more numerous, more warlike people – Bantu-speaking tribes with refined military systems and, because they kept livestock and tilled the soil, an appetite for land. Some groups of Bushmen were simply wiped out, the men killed and, often, the women taken captive, so introducing Bushman genes into a substantial part of the subcontinent's ethnic composition (and into its culture: the 'click' in some of the languages and much of the animistic beliefs of traditional black societies are of Bushman origin). Others took to a coastal lifestyle, forsaking the fruits of the hunt for those of the sea. Yet others, a small proportion, were left alone to pursue their ancient ways because they had made their homes in the immensity of the northern wastelands, the Kalahari regions, in which only they, with their simple needs and special skills, could survive.

The other branch of the family, the Hottentots, virtually ceased to exist as a coherent society after white settlement. Many, probably most, succumbed to savage outbreaks of smallpox and other alien epidemics of the eighteenth century. Some of the survivors moved inland to become the half-breed Korana, Griqua and Oorlam groups. Others remained as 'Colonial Hottentots' and, after the abolition of slavery in the 1830s, mixed with the new freemen, adding their progeny to what eventually became known as the Cape coloured community. Today only a few groups, notably the Nama people of the south-western region of the country and in Namibia, retain an identity clearly traceable to their Hottentot origins.

THE COMING OF THE WHITE MAN

In August 1487 two 100-ton caravels and a small store-ship, under the command of Bartolomeu Dias, hoisted full sail in the mouth of the Tagus River and set a south-westerly course into the Atlantic. Sixteen months later Dias was back in Portugal, without any great treasures but in the certain and profoundly valuable knowledge that his ships had rounded the southern tip of Africa. The sea-route to India and the spice-rich Molucca islands was, at last, open to Portugal's royal fleets.

The curious probability is, though, that his epic voyage was not the first to have taken European explorers around the Cape. Some two thousand years earlier a flotilla of sturdy Phoenician biremes – double-banked galleys – almost certainly accomplished this feat. Their captains had been charged by Pharaoh Necho to sail down the east coast – that is to say, through the Red Sea and past Zanzibar – and to 'come back through the Pillars of Hercules to the Northern Sea and so to Egypt'. This they duly did and reported, according to the Greek historian Herodotus, 'a thing which I cannot believe, but another man may, namely, in sailing round Libya [the ancient name for Africa] they had the sun on their right hand'. In other words they had coasted westwards past Cape Point.

However that may be, it was the Portuguese of the fifteenth and sixteenth centuries who, 'in the service of God our Lord and to our own advantage', pioneered the modern trade routes. Armed with the most rudimentary of navigational aids – a mariner's compass, instruments to gauge wind direction and an astrolabe to determine latitude – their talented admirals set out to find and chart the sea lane to the treasure-troves of the east. Diego Cão negotiated the arid Namib coast, reaching a point just north of present-day Swakopmund in 1486. Two years later Dias ran into the notorious Cape south-easter, allowed his ships to be driven a thousand miles and more into the Atlantic Ocean; then set course first southwards and finally north-east to make his landfall at Mossel Bay – a prodigious exercise in navigational acrobatics that had taken him past the Cape of Storms.

The way was now open, though Dias would enjoy little of the glory: at Algoa Bay, site of modern Port Elizabeth, the votes of his less intrepid travelling companions went against him and he was forced to turn back. It was left to the strong-willed, supremely confident Vasco da Gama, four years later, to chart a course up the Natal coast to the busy Islamic outposts of Mozambique, where his 'ships of the Franks' caused some consternation, and thence across the Indian Ocean to Malabar and beyond.

Thereafter, for over a century, the Iberian commercial empire (Portugal and Spain were unified by dynastic marriage in 1580) flourished, providing both a magnet for and a challenge to other, increasingly enterprising, maritime powers. Of these, certainly insofar as the Cape sea-lanes to India were concerned, the Dutch were to emerge as the leaders.

For much of the sixteenth century the hard-headed merchants of the Netherlands acted as middlemen in the lucrative spice trade, distributing the precious merchandise throughout a Europe enjoying renascent prosperity, legitimate contributors to business life, welcomed by both supplier and customer. Less legitimate were the freebooters, who scoured the seas in their swift, well-armed ships in search of the easy pickings provided by galleons heavily laden with the wealth of the Indies and the Americas. But, generally speaking, relations between Antwerp and Lisbon remained amicable enough, until the last decade of the century. Then, for a number of reasons related to the unification of Portugal and Spain, the Dutch decided to go it alone, and to deal directly with the Spice Islands.

Successful reconnaissance expeditions were mounted in the 1590s by the brothers De Houtman and by Jan van Linschoten, whose five-year odyssey produced a rich volume of hitherto secret information on the Portuguese trade and trading regions, all of which he consolidated into his *Itinerario*, published in 1595 and soon to become a kind of mercantile and navigational bible for Holland's seafaring fraternity. Between 1595 and 1602 rival Dutch companies, now competing in earnest for the Moluccan connection, sent a series of fleets to the East Indies, their voyages involving a longer haul across the Indian Ocean than the traditional Portuguese route from Mozambique to Malabar on the Indian subcontinent. The Cape and its watering places therefore became increasingly significant in the calculations of the Dutch navigators.

Both Mossel Bay, which Dias had named *Angra de São Bras*, and Table Bay, known then as Saldanha Bay (the name now belongs to a rocky embayment some 100 kilometres to the north), had been used by Portuguese and other admirals for the past hundred years as incidental ports of call, natural harbours where there was shelter from storm and where emergency repairs could be ef-

fected, fresh water taken from the perennial springs and provisions bought by barter. Indeed, as early as 1501 one devout commander, João da Nova, had erected a small stone church at *São Bras*, the first European building to be constructed on what is now South African soil. It was to be half a century, though, before any Dutchman thought of establishing a permanent presence on the southern shore.

In due course the competing interests within Holland's mercantile world sank their differences and united under the federal umbrella of the Dutch East India Company, formally incorporated, and granted its charter by the States General of the Netherlands in 1602. During the decades that followed, the Company, which had a directorate grandly known as 'The Lords Seventeen', created a maritime empire that elevated tiny Holland to the highest ranks of Europe's nation states. It established a sophisticated administration in the Malayan Archipelago and, after 1619, a permanent far-eastern headquarters at Batavia, Java, the whole supported by a spreading network of garrisoned trading stations called comptoirs.

The Company's decision to create a comptoir at the Cape was more the result of accident than forethought. In 1647 the *Nieuw Haerlem* foundered on the shores of Table Bay and, although the captain and most of the crew were taken on to Holland aboard another vessel – part of a fleet whose passenger-list included one Jan van Riebeeck – some 60 sailors, under command of junior merchant Leendert Janszen, remained behind, sheltered from the elements by a crude fort built of wood salvaged from the wreck.

On his return a full year later Janszen submitted his *Remonstrantie*, a report strongly urging the Company to establish a victualling post at the Cape: a station that would trade peaceably with the local Hottentot community, and supply fresh produce to the scurvy-ridden crews bound to and from the East Indies.

On the strength of Janszen's submission, and a carefully argued second opinion by Jan van Riebeeck – the 32-year-old former Company employee who had walked the slopes of Table Mountain a year before and who was now anxious to re-enter Company service – the decision was taken. Scarcely a momentous one in the context of the Dutch East India Company's overall, immense operations – just another small fort manned by a hundred or so men, and this one at the southern end of an unknown land that, according to one jaundiced seafarer, 'yielded nothing to delight the heart of man'. Van Riebeeck was appointed commander, and his instructions drawn up. Modestly, and without fanfare, the expedition sailed out of Texel on 24 December, 1651.

THE FIRST SETTLEMENT

In the practical, somewhat prosaic minds of the Lords Seventeen there was no thought of colonizing the Cape, let alone a vision of creating a European Christian state on the African continent. Their aims were commercial and limited. Nevertheless, a century and a half after the landing of Van Riebeeck, when the Dutch finally relinquished control, the makings of such a state did exist. The frontiers of white settlement had been pushed 500 kilometres to the east and 100 kilometres of prosperous farmland and vineyards lay to the north and north-east. By 1806, when the British assumed control for the second time, Cape Town was a busy seaport, host to ships of a score of nations and the seat of a sophisticated administration. South Africa was a reality – an uncomfortable one, even then, for the clash of cultures, a foretaste of future conflict, was already in evidence. There was antagonism between Boer and Briton, between black and white and, always, the competitive struggle for land. The process had been put in motion, and was irreversible.

Nor did Van Riebeeck, the first commander, have aspirations beyond his immediate, functional task. His instructions, which he carried out with solid Dutch thoroughness, were quite specific: he was to provide for passing ships of the Company 'the means of procuring herbs, flesh, water and other needful refreshments – and by this means restore the health of the sick'. He was also to build a fort 'in order to take possession at the Cape and so that you cannot be surprised by anyone'.

Van Riebeeck's three little vessels, *Drommedaris* (his flagship), the *Reijger* and the *Goede Hoop*, nosed their way into Table Bay on the blustery evening of 6 April, 1652. Three days later the Commander had personally marked out the fort's site, and by 21 April the first rough walls were up and supporting five cannon. The project, however, was to be plagued by set-back after set-back – the eastern ramparts simply could not withstand the driving winter rainstorms. Indeed, for the first few months in this new and hostile land, life was barely tolerable. As the store of basic foodstuffs – rice, groats, flour and dried beans – ran low, the settlers yearningly watched for a sail on the horizon, for a Company ship bringing replenishments. During the final, uncomfortable weeks before help came, they were reduced to a diet of salted penguin. And they were nervous: sleep at night, according to one of the party, was broken by 'the roaring of many sea-cows, lions, tigers and other wild animals'.

While the fort was being built, the Garden was also taking shape. Eight gardeners had been brought along, but in fact almost everyone lent a hand. Despite the appalling conditions of life and weather, they managed to plant peas, beans, fennel, lettuce, endive and radish. The Cape is not always at its best in April and May: the settlers had to dig and build in downpours of icy rain which ruined most of the first crops. Caterpillars and blight put paid to the rest. And not only did plants succumb to disease: dysentery, together with a number of other ailments, attacked the small community. Among those who fell ill were the surgeon and his assistant, and it was fortunate for everyone that Van Riebeeck had once served as a ship's doctor and could tend the sufferers himself. There were Hottentot raids. Life was precarious.

But the chain of catastrophes came to an end, and fortune at last began to smile on the exiles. The long-awaited ships arrived. Sheep and cattle began to breed. Lemon and apple trees, brought by the relieving fleet, were planted, and for those more interested in the elixir of the grape and hop, the Cape's first tavern – run by Annetje Boom, wife of the settlement's chief gardener – opened. It did not lack for customers.

In fact, Van Riebeeck was soon looking with a somewhat rueful eye at the number of ships sailing into Table Bay, their seamen making serious inroads into the community's slender resources. The lower ranks did pay their way (though money was not all that relevant when meat and vegetables were none too plentiful for the residents themselves), but the Commander was obliged to entertain important visitors himself, and noted with irritation that his personal table cutlery was disappearing at a steady rate, no doubt to be treasured as souvenirs by his erstwhile guests.

Jan van Riebeeck left the Cape for Batavia in 1662 and was succeeded by Commander Zacharias Wagenaar. Four years later, the building of Cape Town's sturdy Castle began. It was to be a full decade before the stronghold was complete, even though, in the early stages, pretty well everyone helped in the work, including the Commander himself, his wife and small son, who carried baskets of earth to the ramparts. At the end of the first day's work a feast was given: it consisted in part of six sheep and two oxen, and one of the settlers read a poem to the effect that neither Augustus nor Julius Caesar had laid, as they had done that day, 'a corner stone at the far end of the earth'.

PUTTING DOWN ROOTS

Among the Company's many injunctions to Van Riebeeck, one proved especially difficult to accommodate in the first years of the settlement – that it should be self-supporting. As the workload increased, so more officials arrived, putting such severe pressure on the community's modest larder that within two years ships anchored in Table Bay were off-loading more supplies than they were taking on.

Van Riebeeck's solution represented a radical change in policy: he turned to private enterprise, releasing a number of men from their Company contracts to set themselves up as independent farmers and tradesmen. Other 'free-burgher' families arrived from Holland.

The results were immediate and gratifying. In its very first, experimental, year – 1656 – the block of land set aside at Rondebosch produced a bumper crop of wheat, enough for local needs with some to spare. A small beginning, perhaps, but a significant one – the Cape was now no longer a commercial garrison with strictly limited objectives but a permanent colony capable of growth. The move marked the start of the settlement proper.

Over the years the free-burghers grew in number, steadily pushing out the frontiers – to the Hottentot Hollands region in the 1670s and to Stellenbosch nine years later. This charming little centre was the brainchild of and named after Simon van der Stel, the half-caste, outstandingly innovative Governor of the Cape from 1679 to the century's end. He had earmarked the district as an ideal wheat-producing area, and the farms which were established there paid such handsome dividends that within a short while there was an over-supply of corn and the emphasis was shifted to the growing of grapes and the making of wine.

Not that this was a new idea: Jan van Riebeeck himself took a deep interest in viticulture and, a mere month after setting foot ashore in 1652, had placed an order with Amsterdam for seeds and plants 'and also vines which ought to thrive as well on local hill slopes as they do in Spain and France'. He received Muscadel, Fransdruif (Spanish Palomino) and Hanepoot (Muscat d'Alexandrie), and by 2 February, 1659 was able to confide to his journal that 'Today, praise be to God, wine can be made for the first time from Cape Grapes, namely from the new must fresh from the vat'. The first vineyard, on his private farm Boscheuvel (now Bishopscourt) contained just 12 000 vines; thirty years later the grape harvests had spread their gracious mantle over much of the hinterland. By 1750 there were four million vines growing around the pretty towns of Stellenbosch, Paarl and Franschhoek, yielding an annual flow of 12 000 hectolitres of wine.

People came to make their home in the new land. Most of them were Dutch, though there was a sprinkling of Belgians, Scandinavians and, especially, Germans. By the time the whites of the Cape numbered around a thousand, in 1688, they were joined by a group of most welcome immigrants – the sober and industrious Huguenots. These were French Protestants who, after the Edict of Nantes was revoked and they were threatened with religious persecution, fled to pastures new and far – the farther away, they felt, the better. There were 164 of them: a fine shot-in-the-arm for the small community which, by then, had suffered harassment and direct attack by Hottentots (the five tribes of the area numbered an intimidating 14 000).

The first Cape homes were modest, single-storeyed, flat-roofed affairs of sun-dried brick, the white-washed walls and green-painted woodwork lending a certain charm to the town. In the country areas the settlers built more substantial homes, often of stone, reed-thatched, thick-walled and entirely functional. With prosperity, though, a distinctive style began to evolve during the latter part of the century: gabled, half-shuttered houses, the entrance-way an impressive focal point through which one walked into a spacious *voorhuis*. These farmsteads were built symmetrically, even severely, to 'T', 'H', and 'U' patterns. As the decades passed, the cold lines of the grander ones were softened with the addition of wings, and courtyards were encircled by outbuildings. Thus emerged the renowned Cape Dutch architectural idiom, some lovely examples of which still grace the Peninsula and particularly its northern and eastern hinterland.

With time, too, the gable changed, taking on a bewildering variety of shapes, plain and rounded giving way to convoluted convex-concave; to classical; and to the elaborately ornate, thick edge-mouldings sweeping across in swirls and scrolls and curlicues. Eventually, and unhappily, this most distinctive of features became little more than an ugly and irrelevant appendage to the worst kind of run-of-the-mill South African suburban home.

Curiously enough, many of the early architectural elements, including the gable, derived not from Holland but from the East and were introduced by Malay slaves skilled in building crafts. Slavery, indeed, was a prominent aspect of Cape community life for almost 200 years. The early settlers were inhibitively short of labour, both skilled and unskilled; Van Riebeeck felt reluctant to conscript the local Hottentots, valuing their goodwill (they were, in any case, considered to be 'unreliable' – perhaps because of their cheerfully independent characters), and a formal decision to import slaves was taken in the 1660s. The system was an iniquitous one in retrospect, but not exclusive to the Cape: slave-trading and owning was common practice in much of the world until the 1830s and later; across the Atlantic a civil war was fought over the issue in the 1860s. The first slave to appear was a stowaway from Batavia who arrived in March 1653, but slavery really began five years later when, in 1668, the *Amersfoort* acquired 170 slaves from a Portuguese ship and off-loaded them at Table Bay.

Thereafter, demand from wheat- and wine-farming free-burghers ensured a steady growth in numbers, despite the cost (up to 100 *gulden* per slave) and the high incidence of runaways. By 1710 there were about 1 200 adult slaves at the Cape; in 1795, when the British took over, the figure had risen to 17 000 – a number somewhat in excess of the white population. They were brought, originally, from places as far afield as Guinea and Angola on Africa's west coast, Delagoa Bay on the east, as well as from Madagascar, Java and, especially, Malaya. After the initial influx, importation dwindled to a trickle: children born to slave parents accounted for the steady growth rate.

THE ROAD TO THE EAST

Like any frontier community, the early Cape settlers had their share of enterprising explorers. Forays into the northern interior were launched in the first few years by Wintervogel (who reached present-day Malmesbury); Gabbema (the Berg River Valley and Paarl, which he named after the giant granite boulders that dominate the area – depending on the light they often gleam like pearls); Danckaert (the Cedarberg and Olifants River – named after a herd of 300 elephant he saw); Van Meerhoff (Namaqualand). Van der Stel himself led an expedition to the copper mountains of Namaqualand in 1685. A hundred years after Van Riebeeck's landing Jacobus Coetsee, a captain of the burgher dragoons, crossed the Orange River and wandered over the high plateau for some months.

The eastern horizons were broadened by, among others, Hieronimus Cruse in the late 1660s: he trekked overland to Mossel Bay and heard tell of 'darker-skinned men' – that is to say, the Xhosa, who were by then long settled along the east coast and were advancing southwards. Shortly afterwards the settlers got to know more about these mysterious black people with the stranding, in 1686, of the Dutch ship *Stavenisse* south of the future Port Natal on the east coast: the rescue parties produced eyewitness accounts of the Xhosa around the Kei River.

Settlement of the eastern districts received its first major impetus when, in 1699, Governor Willem Adriaan van der Stel (Simon's second son) reversed Company policy, which had hitherto discouraged stock-farmers from trekking. Throughout the eighteenth century the frontiers were pushed steadily outwards to the north and east by the relentless advance of trekboers – nomadic farmers moving farther and farther away from the restrictions of government. New magisterial districts, each controlled by an official known as a landdrost, were established as the virgin land was tamed and homesteads were built. In 1745 a new drostdy – as the regional headquarters of the landdrost was called – was established in the attractive little village which, two years later, was to be named Swellendam. By mid-century the boundary of the Cape of Good Hope had reached the Great Brak River near Mossel Bay and farms were appearing as far away as the west bank of the Gamtoos. By the 1780s settlers had moved farther eastwards and were putting down their roots along the Great Fish River; before the decade was out the town and district of Graaff-Reinet had been formally proclaimed.

By this time the central administration in Cape Town was at acrimonious odds with the farther reaches of its eastern domains. Ruggedly individualistic frontiersmen, resenting distant and what they regarded as misguided control over their economic life, and the Company's handling of the Xhosa problem, declared (briefly) their own independent republics, Graaff-Reinet in February 1795 and Swellendam four months later.

In fact the physical power of the Dutch East India Company, and therefore the strength of its administrative muscle in the regions, had been declining since the early 1700s. Towards the end of the century, after four debilitating Anglo-Dutch wars, France and England had emerged as the leading European protagonists, rivals in the quest for, among other things, control of the oceans. The Cape, weakly garrisoned and strategically positioned on the sea-routes, was a tempting prize. British troops landed at Muizenberg in July 1795, but six weeks were to pass before the local militia could be defeated at Wynberg Hill. The capitulation, signed at Rondebosch on 16 September, inaugurated a period of direct rule from Whitehall that, with one brief break, was to underpin events on the subcontinent for the next hundred years and more – until the Act of Union of 1910 created the all-but-sovereign state of South Africa.

THE BRITISH PRESENCE

The country that the English soldiers took over was still very much a backwater in the flow of international affairs. True, Cape Town had grown, but at the end of the eighteenth century it still comprised little more than a cluster of 2 000 or so houses that sprawled from jettied dockside up and around the lower slopes of Table Mountain. Along the Liesbeek River there were a few still-rural villages that were later to become the swathe of suburbia stretching from Woodstock to Wynberg; farther afield lay a hinterland of prosperous wheat and wine farms, and the remote and troubled eastern border area.

The town itself was attractive enough, its pride the Gardens, started by Van Riebeeck as a prosaic vegetable patch but now assuming a more decorative rôle. Indeed as early as 1685 the visiting scholar Abbé de Choisy could observe that he 'would have liked to see it in a corner of Versailles'. Oaks and ashes shaded its

THE AGE OF THE GENERALS. In 1910 the two former republics of the Transvaal and the Orange Free State came together with the British colonies of the Cape and Natal to form the Union of South Africa, and for the next four decades – years of war abroad and sporadic rebellion at home, of both economic depression and industrial progress – the political arena was dominated by three Afrikaners, all of whom had fought with distinction against the British during the Anglo-Boer War. Louis Botha and Jan Smuts were statesmen, 'Empire men' who practised the politics of reconciliation; Barry Hertzog a dedicated nationalist whose ideological heirs would eventually, in 1948, grasp and hold the reins of power on behalf of Afrikanerdom.

Members of the National Convention (1) which created the Union constitution. Union celebrations in Cape Town, 1910 (2). Mohandas Gandhi (3 left) laboured long, hard and with only partial success for Indian rights in South Africa. Alfred Lord Milner (4), architect of the Anglo-Boer War and chief engineer of a post-war reconstruction programme that paved the way for a united South Africa. Black land rights and taxation were the elements that triggered the Bambata Rebellion – an uprising of some 6 000 Zulu people – in 1906. Colonial troops are pictured (5) executing rebels. General Louis Botha (6), the Union's first premier and commander-in-chief of its forces, with his staff during the First World War. Botha had first to quell an anti-British white rebellion at home before leading his army in the conquest of German South West Africa: picture (8) shows the raising of the Union Jack over the Rathaus at Windhoek. Mounted police clear Rissik Street, Johannesburg (9) during the 1922 'Red Revolt', a violent reaction by white miners to the threat posed by cheap black labour on the Witwatersrand. Barry Hertzog (7). In 1939 South Africa again joined the Allied cause against Germany, her troops – all volunteers – campaigning successfully in East Africa, the Western Desert and Italy. Shown here is a recruiting station in Adderley Street, Cape Town (10). Field Marshal Smuts at No. 10 Downing Street (11) with Winston Churchill shortly after the German surrender on 8 May 1945.

more mundane plants; a pleasure lodge had been added in 1700 (later, some think, rebuilt to become Government House, now known as the Tuynhuis). There was a menagerie at the mountain end; fine buildings, including the Old Supreme Court, which had started life as the Slave Lodge, had made their appearance. Leading from harbour to garden was the elegant, stone-paved, oak-lined Heerengracht – present-day Adderley Street. The land beyond the quaint old harbour area was much later to be reclaimed from the sea and now supports many of Cape Town's modern city blocks and dockland.

Other features contributed substance and, if not sophistication, certainly charm to the place: the leisurely spaciousness of the Grand Parade; some beautiful private residences, the Cape style perhaps best exemplified by the pleasantly solid Koopmans de Wet House on Strand Street; the massive Castle on what was then the waterfront, and of course the town's busy, warren-like dockland. Cape Town had become one of the foremost ports of the southern hemisphere, host to ships and sailors of a dozen nations and already famed as the 'tavern of the seas', its clubs and pubs proliferating, its streets alive with horse-drawn traffic and the press of polyglot humanity.

Indeed, as colonial headquarters went, the new British administrators could have been a great deal worse off. They settled themselves in comfortably after the second occupation, in 1806, and addressed the issues of government: slavery; the growing spirit of independence among the Boers of the outlying regions; the agitated Xhosa presence on the eastern border; the need to economize (Britain had incurred a huge war debt during the Napoleonic struggles), and the sparseness of the frontier settler community.

In 1806 the colony's population comprised 26 000 whites, some 30 000 slaves, 20 000 Hottentots and uncountable numbers of Bushmen and Bantu-speaking people beyond the Great Fish River, posing a constant threat to the miniscule border farming settlements.

The first full-scale Frontier War had erupted in 1779; altogether, there would be eight more over the next hundred years and during this time the border was moved progressively eastwards to the Kei River. Of these series of frontier skirmishes, probably the most significant was the fifth, in 1819, when the Xhosa army mounted a direct attack on Grahamstown. This was repulsed by the garrison but the event convinced Governor Lord Charles Somerset that only massive immigration could bring any semblance of stability to the troubled border areas.

Conviction was translated into action with the landing in Algoa Bay, in 1820, of 60 parties of English, Scots and Irish families numbering some 4 000 men, women and children – a small fraction of the 90 000 who had applied to emigrate but enough, the authorities decided, to populate and pacify the recently proclaimed Albany district of the eastern Cape – the vast area covering most of the disputed territory between the Bushmans and Great Fish rivers and from Grahamstown to the coast.

From Algoa Bay the newcomers were moved inland by oxwagon (at their own expense) in blissful ignorance of the almost impossible conditions that awaited them. Warning bells sounded clear, however, when they took leave of Colonel Cuyler, landdrost (magistrate) of Uitenhage, who had accompanied them part of the way. 'Gentlemen', he said, 'when you go out to plough, never leave your guns at home.' It dawned on them that they were to serve not only as pioneers but also as a kind of plain-clothes militia, and in a short while they would also discover that battle with the desolate land would test their courage and endurance even more than that against the Xhosa.

Their troubles were complex and legion, perhaps most poignantly summed up in a letter from one Captain Buller, written during the first season. He said: 'My wheat, two months ago the most promising I ever saw in any country, is now cut down and in heaps for burning. . . The rust has utterly destroyed it; not a grain have we saved. My barley, from the drought, and a grub which attacks the blade, produced little more than I sowed. My Indian corn, very much injured by the caterpillar; cabbages destroyed by the lice; the beans all scorched by the hot wind. . . Our cows are all dry from want of grass; not the least appearance of verdure as far as the eye can reach. Nothing but one great wilderness of faded grass. On Saturday whilst watching by the sick bed of my dear little girl (she had been bitten by a snake while running over the veld without shoes and stockings, and died), I was startled by the cry of wild dogs. I ran to the window and saw about thirty of these ferocious animals; before I could drive them off, they had killed twenty of my flock, which consisted of twenty-seven in all. I stood for a moment thinking of my misery, my dying child, my blasted crops, my scattered and ruined flock. God's will be done. I have need of fortitude to bear up against such accumulation of misery. Farewell. . .'

The settlers suffered five years of bitter hardship and disappointment on the unforgiving land: conditions were primitive; equipment rudimentary; the allotments too small; the ban on recruiting labour from among the Xhosa clans a prohibitive restriction; the depredations of drought, locust and tribesman an unrelenting menace. Few survived as farmers, most of them drifting into the villages and small towns, originally military garrisons, that now studded the eastern Cape countryside.

Nevertheless, the pioneer scheme was not a total failure in the context of the British colonial administration's priorities, high among which was the creation of a white-inhabited 'buffer' region in the east. Four thousand new settlers might not seem a very substantial number by modern standards, but it increased the area's population by a full ten per cent. Moreover, things improved dramatically in the decade after 1825. It saw more freedom of movement, bigger farms and a general relaxation of bureaucratic restriction and the introduction, by the settlers, of a sheep-farming industry that was to become the country's principal agricultural activity and the mainstay of the eastern Cape economy, ushered in a welcome era of prosperity and growth.

Towards the end of the 1830s, too, an organized community of Britons put its first, tentative roots down on the far eastern coast.

Since 1834 there had been a small trading post at Port Natal – founded by the enterprising Lieutenant Francis Farewell – and white hunters stalked the thickly wooded hinterland in search of elephant and ivory. They were tolerated, even welcomed, by the powerful Zulu king Shaka. They were transients rather than colonists, even if they did hold land – 9 000 square kilometres around the bay – under a royal, though vague, grant. The status of the settlement changed with the arrival of the missionary and magistrate Allen Gardiner, who called a meeting on 23 June, 1835 to proclaim a township. At the inaugural get-together, Gardiner remembered, 'almost total silence was observed. . . At length a voice cried out: "Now let's go and settle the bounds". . . Being the winter season, it was a sort of union of hunters, who, tired of chasing sea-cows and buffalo, were now sighing for town houses and domestic cheer. . .'

It was in this casual, impromptu fashion that Durban, later to become South Africa's premier port and third city, was founded. During the course of the nineteenth century, large-scale immigration schemes ensured both its growth and Natal's quintessentially English character, but for the first decade or so the settlement remained small and vulnerable, its affairs intimately bound up with the eastern prong of the Great Trek.

THE OUTWARD URGE

In the mid-1830s there began an exodus of Boers from the volatile eastern Cape. Families gathered in parties, inspanned their oxen and headed into the immense and little-known northern and north-eastern interior armed with scarcely more than musket, Bible and faith in their destiny.

The migration, apparently spontaneous in its initial thrust but in fact well organized, started in a fairly modest way, gathered momentum over the next few turbulent years and eventually, when the sound of battle had died away and the wanderers became farmers again, succeeded in doubling the area of white settlement in Africa.

Arguments about the nature of the Great Trek are numerous and conflicting. To the dispassionate historian it was just one more movement of peoples in search of *lebensraum* in a century characterized by mass-migrations, comparable perhaps to the westward advance of the American pioneers. To the Afrikaners it remains a heroic saga, fount of their republican traditions and of their national identity. To British officialdom of the time and later it was a catastrophe, the origin of a divided country: the trigger for deep and lasting dissension between Boer, Briton and black people. To blacks the Trek must have appeared simply as a blatant exercise in physical conquest. What is not in dispute is that, in the end, the Afrikaner nation did manage to occupy huge territories between the Orange and the Limpopo, to establish independent republics and, ultimately, to wage a long and bitter war against the British Empire. It was, without doubt, the most crucial event in the story of modern South Africa.

Much has been said of the Trek's causes: of the ruinous losses suffered by Boer homesteaders in the exposed eastern frontier region during their never-ending struggle for land against the Xhosa; of lack of military support from the British authorities in Cape Town; of the colonial government's 'over-reactive' respect for the status and rights of black people, inspired by philanthropists in London and Scottish missionaries in Africa; of the abolition of slavery; and above all of British meddling in and control over the affairs of independent-minded frontiersmen. The essence of the whole matter was more simply, if rather ruggedly, explained to an English resident of Bathurst in the 1830s. The Boer said that 'in his father's lifetime and his own they had been five times clean swept out by [Xhosa raiders]. . . that for protection, the future would be like the past, indeed he thought they were worse off than fifty years ago; in those old times when they were robbed they redressed the matter themselves, but now their hands were tied while [the Xhosa's] were loose'.

There was, though, a more positive side: the Boer people were not simply running away from an intolerable situation, they were moving towards what they perceived as their Promised Land. They knew a little of what lay in the vast interior: earlier migrants had preceded them, individual *trekboers* who had wandered the northern veld for generations in search of better grazing and hunting-grounds. From the information that filtered back the prospects of finding peace and solitude appeared bright enough to merit exploration, if for no other reason than that immense swathes of fertile territory were being almost entirely, tragically, depopulated as a consequence of what is known as the *Difaqane*.

To digress a little from the Great Trek (though the two events were closely interactive), the *Difaqane*, in its simplest definition, was the forced migration of millions of black tribesmen, initially to the west and north of Zululand and eventually over most of the northern subcontinent. It began when Shaka, leader of the Zulus and warrior supreme, cleared his immediate neighbourhood of all opposition and set out on the bloody road of conquest, igniting a

massive chain reaction of violence and counter-violence. Defeated tribes would move on, displacing others, who in turn migrated to spread fire, sword and famine in farther reaches. It was the domino principle in classic and devastating action. To cite three examples:

☐ Shaka launched his first attack on Matiwane's powerful Ngwane clan in the eastern foothills of the Drakensberg. Matiwane moved on southwards and westwards, to assault the southern Nguni and the Sotho of the uplands, who scattered to cause havoc elsewhere.

☐ Mzilikazi, perhaps Shaka's most enterprising general, quarrelled with his king and fled north with an army that grew as he conquered and absorbed tribe after tribe. His cataclysmically destructive path led him to the Olifants River and then westwards into Sotho territory. Eventually he was defeated in the Transvaal by a mixed force of trekkers, Hottentots and Tswana, and moved on, across the Limpopo River, to establish the Matabele empire.

☐ Two other groups were founded by disaffected Zulu commanders: Soshangane, who led his *impis* into Mozambique (the Shangaans); and Zwangendaba, who settled 2 000 kilometres to the north, around Lake Malawi (the Angoni).

Meanwhile, the Boers trekked, first in their hundreds and then in their thousands. The story is complex to the point where, certainly within the scope of this brief narrative, it defies meaningful synthesis. However, it can perhaps be divided into two broad segments:

First, a substantial element of the trekkers saw Natal as their ultimate haven. Groups of these crossed the Orange and, by the middle of 1837, had gathered at a place between Thaba Nchu and the Vet River from where an advance party, led by Piet Retief, set off eastwards towards Durban and beyond, into Zululand. Shaka's successor, Dingane, received Retief with deceptive amiability and by December the main body of trekkers, encouraged by the promise of land south of the Tugela River, had hauled their wagons over the high Drakensberg, and were in Natal.

After concluding the formal treaty, however, Retief and his pathfinder party of 69 were murdered on the instructions of Dingane, who went on to attack the trekkers in a series of fierce engagements at Bloukrans, Weenen and elsewhere. (Durban was also invested: the fledgling settlement – about 30 whites – took refuge aboard ship.)

The trekkers had suffered grievous casualties but by mid-December 1838 they had managed to rally their forces. On 16 December, 1838, after a night spent in prayer and in the offering of the formal vow, or covenant, at a place now known as Blood River, their muskets and laagered discipline routed the Zulu army.

The Boer Republic of Natalia was destined to be short-lived. In May 1842 British troops occupied Durban, were besieged by the Boers but succeeded in summoning reinforcements (this was the occasion of Dick King's renowned 1 500-kilometre ride to enlist the help of the garrison of Grahamstown) and the four-year-old State disintegrated. Some of the Boers returned to the Cape, most rejoined the main body of northern Voortrekkers.

These had in the meantime been busy preparing the way for settlement of the land beyond the Orange River. During the next decade numerous small groups of hardy pioneers took their wagon-trains over enormous tracts of inhospitable country, suffering hardship, privation and, some of them, death along the way. Heat and drought, disease, the ravages of wild animals and confrontation with the black tribes, all took their toll. Andries Potgieter's party pushed the farthest north, crossing the Limpopo into present-day Zimbabwe as early as 1836. Van Rensburg's was annihilated in Mozambique. Louis Trichardt's odyssey took him first to the northern Transvaal's Soutpansberg and then south-east through fever-ridden Mozambique to Delagoa Bay (modern Maputo). Here both he and his wife died and the remnants of his decimated group took ship to Durban.

By the mid-1850s, however, the Boers had settled in sufficient numbers to warrant the establishment and formal recognition of two viable independent states, one between the Orange and the Vaal rivers, the other between the Vaal and the Limpopo.

TWO REPUBLICS, TWO COLONIES

From about the middle of the nineteenth century onwards southern Africa comprised four major and a number of less substantial political entities. They inter-acted, of course, but for the most part functioned separately, and continued to do so until Union in 1910. The web of events is intricate. In broad outline, however:
□ The country that was to become the Orange Free State – that is to say, the land between the Orange and the Vaal – had been infiltrated by a few trekboers during the early pioneering years, but it was only with the northward advance of the Voortrekkers from 1835 that white settlement began in earnest. The small township of Winburg (named in commemoration of the Boer victory over Mzilikazi's marauders at the Battle of Vechtkop), was founded in 1837 as the 'capital' of the new territory. This decision turned out to be somewhat premature since the trekkers were still too divided to form a coherent state. Their lack of unity, and a confusing element of black-white confrontation over land rights and frontiers, prompted the British to annex the area and to create the Orange River Sovereignty in 1848. Bloemfontein, then scarcely more than a schoolroom and a cluster of white-washed cottages, was declared the administrative centre and headquarters of the British Resident.

None of these events succeeded in bringing stability to the region (at one point the Boers rose in revolt, and were defeated by a force commanded by the Cape Governor, Sir Harry Smith). Finally, though, following the Bloemfontein Convention in 1854, Britain recognized the independence of the new Republic of the Orange Free State. Real progress was achieved under the steady guidance of Jan Brand, President for the 24 crucial and crisis-ridden years between 1864 and 1888. Brand accepted British dominance on the subcontinent but stoically resisted moves, principally by Lord Carnarvon, the Colonial Secretary, to bring about a confederation of southern African states. However, the discovery of diamond-fields in the northern Cape in 1867 brought prosperity and political muscle, both of which were reinforced with the arrival of the railway in 1888 and the customs agreement with the Cape a year later.
□ The Transvaal's constitutional course was similar, though from the very beginning its settlers tended to be less tractable, more hostile to British influence than those of the Orange Free State. Many of the Boer intransigents, for instance, crossed the Vaal into the northern bastion after the Battle of Boomplaats in 1848.

Independence was conferred on the Transvaal, or more correctly the South African Republic, at the Sand River Convention of 1852. Four years later, despite religious controversy and a great deal of quarrelsome rivalry among the local leaders (much of the territory had been carved up into mini-republics), the State finally managed to elect its first president, Marthinus Pretorius, and adopt a formal constitution. Significantly, it was officially declared that the people of the South African Republic 'desire to permit no equality between Coloured people and the white inhabitants, either in Church or State'. The attractive little town of Pretoria, set in the beautiful rolling countryside of the Highveld and named after the hero of Blood River, became the capital.

During the confederation issue of the late 1870s the Transvaal, predictably, proved the most isolationist of the four white communities, a fact which may have contributed to its formal annexation by British troops under the Natal Secretary for Native Affairs, Sir Theophilus Shepstone, in 1877 (the official reason given for the occupation was fear of open conflict between Zulu and Transvaler – a reason which became invalid after the Zulu empire was finally crushed at Ulundi in 1879). On 16 December, 1880 the Boer leaders, who now included one Paul Kruger, re-proclaimed their republic, and went to war. Three months later, on the bloody slopes of Majuba Hill, their forces inflicted the first and only defeat suffered by Britain during the whole of Queen Victoria's long reign. Shortly afterwards, at the Convention of Pretoria, the right to internal self-government was restored to the South African Republic.

Majuba marked one more step on the road to the collapse of Boer-Briton accommodation in southern Africa. For the British, it meant humiliation, and a determination in the corridors of Imperial power to salvage national prestige and pride. For the Boers, it was positive affirmation of their strength as a united people and of their ability to preserve their independence come what may.
□ The Cape, meanwhile, had been progressing as steadily if more sedately towards constitutional maturity.

By the end of the century the eastern and north-eastern borders had stabilized: the former with the establishment of the port of East London and the development of small inland settlements, most starting life as garrisons (King William's Town was one of the more important). The frontiers were finally and formally fixed with the annexation of Pondoland (now part of Transkei) adjoining Natal and, in 1895, of British Bechuanaland (now Botswana), a huge northern wilderness area sprawling between the Transvaal and the Namibia of today. The mountain fortress of Basutoland, which was eventually to become the kingdom of Lesotho, had fallen under the Cape administration in 1871 before reverting to direct British control in 1884.

For 40 years after the First British Occupation the Cape Colony had been ruled, autocratically, by a Whitehall-appointed Governor. In 1834, however, a small concession was made to the democratic process with the appearance of a nominated Legislative Council which included five white colonials. Twenty years later, in 1854, came representative government: a Parliament containing a majority of elected members, but without executive control, which still resided in the office of Governor. This final authority was granted the colonists with the establishment in 1872 of responsible government modelled on the Westminster system, and the institution of a fully elected Parliament with virtually complete powers to conduct the colony's internal affairs. The Imperial voice was henceforth to be heard, chiefly in matters of foreign policy, through an appointed High Commissioner. Qualifications for the franchise were on the basis of income and property rather than colour.
□ The second of nineteenth century southern Africa's self-governing colonies, Natal, had been annexed to the Cape after the demise of the Boer Republic of Natalia in 1844, but became a separate entity, administered by a Lieutenant-Governor, the following year. Towards the end of the decade large-scale immigration schemes stimulated rapid growth during the second half of the century. In 1856 there were 8 000 white settlers in Durban and its lush hinterland (still teeming with wild game: elephants were foraging close to the city well into the twentieth century). By 1893 the figure had risen to 50 000, with Durban shortly to become one of the biggest and busiest ports south of the equator.

Throughout the century, though, and to the present day, the non-white population was in an overwhelming majority. The bulk of this was the Nguni, predominantly the Zulus, who, despite strenuous official efforts to safeguard 'native' land rights, were provoked by white encroachment to the point of open conflict. The Zulu wars culminated in 1879 with the annihilation of a British army at Isandlwana, the heroic sideshow at Rorke's Drift shortly afterwards and the final and decisive defeat of Cetshwayo's regiments at Ulundi. Zululand was ruthlessly balkanized, divided into 13 separate chieftaincies and then, in 1887, annexed to Britain before being incorporated into the Colony of Natal four years later.

The last ethnic ingredient of southern Africa's heterogeneous society was added in the years after the arrival of the first indentured labourers from India in 1860 (*see* page 12). They were followed to Natal's newly-established sugar plantations by a steady stream of Asian migrants. By the turn of the century they, too, outnumbered the colony's white inhabitants.

Thus by the latter half of the 1800s the subcontinent's kaleidoscopic make-up – a mix of peoples of distinct and different identities bound together by history and by geography but of differing cultures and, perhaps inevitably, of conflicting interests – had been established: Briton, Afrikaner and mixed-race in the western Cape; Xhosa and white in the eastern Cape; Zulu, Asian and Briton in Natal; Boer and black in the two republics, with a horde of *uitlanders* – foreigners – poised to invade the about-to-be-discovered gold-fields.

DIAMONDS, GOLD AND WAR

The discovery, in 1867, of the fabulous diamond-fields of Griqualand West, north of the Cape Colony, was a watershed event: it marked the metamorphosis of what had until then been regarded by Britain as a strategically placed backwater, in some respects more a troublesome nuisance than an Imperial asset, into a very valuable colonial possession.

Prospectors, diggers, drifters, chancers and a fair sprinkling of honest men converged on the fields from all parts of the globe, though there was a preponderance of Cape Britons among the men who were to demolish the original diamond hill, create Kimberley's Big Hole and exploit the world's richest source of precious stones.

Problems there were aplenty during the first few frenetic years of the diamond rush: fortunes were made (and lost) overnight; men lit their cigars with ten pound notes, and the champagne flowed, but there was a much seamier side to life in the dusty, unkempt settlement of tents, shacks and the odd brick building. Within a very short time the population of Kimberley exceeded that of Cape Town, but its residents enjoyed practically none of the amenities, civic or social, of the older city. Crime was rife, alcohol and gambling the major preoccupations, and political unrest a sporadic and rowdy feature of the early years (typical was a comic-opera effort to create a 'diggers' republic' and the Black Flag Rebellion of 1875). Britain annexed Griqualand West in 1871, ruled directly for nine years and then, in 1880, incorporated the territory into the Cape Colony. By this time Kimberley had settled down into a more humdrum routine, its respectable air of permanence derived largely from the stability brought to the fields by a young financial genius named Cecil John Rhodes.

Rhodes had emigrated from England as a sickly 19-year-old and made his way without too much delay to the boom town. Within ten years he had consolidated the small-claim workings under his giant De Beers umbrella (and later bought out the flamboyant Barney Barnato's almost-as-substantial holdings) and, by the mid-1880s, was in control of the international diamond trade. This provided the platform from which he would launch his meteoric

career as politician and empire-builder. Already his vision, which encompassed no less than an Africa painted Imperial red from Cape to Cairo, had taken shape in his mind.

Of greater political significance was the accidental discovery, in July 1886, of gold in the Transvaal – the world's biggest field – on the Witwatersrand, just 50 kilometres from the Boer capital Pretoria.

Paul Kruger, now President of the South African Republic, viewed the rapid influx of *uitlanders* with a wary eye. His strained treasury desperately needed the revenue from the mines and from the 'concessions' – monopolies – he liberally granted to suppliers of everything from beer to dynamite, but the newcomers threatened to overwhelm his small and jealously independent burgher state by sheer force of numbers. Johannesburg's *uitlanders*, for their part, began to demand the privileges of citizenship, reasonably at first, then vociferously, and finally violently.

By 1895 the confrontation between the restive English-speaking community, led by a group of mining magnates who called themselves the Reform Committee, on the one hand, and an aging President determined to maintain the Transvaal's Afrikaner identity on the other, had grown to crisis proportions. Early on Monday, 30 December, Dr Leander Starr Jameson and his raiding column of some 700 mounted Rhodesians began their famed but ill-judged ride from the Bechuanaland border towards Pretoria and Johannesburg.

The Jameson Raid was the product of a conspiracy which had four major elements: Cecil Rhodes, now Prime Minister of the Cape Colony and determined to bring the gold-rich Transvaal into the Imperial fold; the Committee, representing the *uitlanders*; Dr Jameson, Rhodes's man in the field, an adventurous soul who appeared to see himself as Clive of India reincarnate; and finally the powerful British Colonial Secretary, Joseph Chamberlain, whose complicity was covert but real enough. Of all these, only the bumbling Reform Committee was inspired by a genuine desire to rectify wrongs; the main aim of the others was straightforward territorial conquest.

The plan, which called for precise synchronization between the Raid and a popular uprising in Johannesburg, misfired badly. Jameson and his men were defeated, captured, tried and convicted (the verdicts were harsh enough, but the leaders served only brief jail sentences).

Anglo-Boer relations plummeted to a new low. All Kruger's suspicions – of Britain's perfidy and her designs on his Republic and its gold – seemed to be confirmed. Indeed they were entirely justified during the next two years. Chamberlain and his representative at the Cape, the arch-Imperialist Alfred Milner, were more set than ever on the 'unification of Southern Africa' – a euphemism for bringing the Transvaal within the British sphere, by negotiation if possible, but by force if necessary. In the long, weary months of diplomatic exchange and conference the Boer leadership tried desperately to avoid the final breach, conceding to Milner's demands for *uitlander* rights only to find, again and again, that there were other, harsher, demands to follow. 'There is no way out except reform in the Transvaal or war,' insisted the High Commissioner. Replied Kruger: 'It is our country you want.' And, on 12 October, 1899, war it was.

Most people – Britain, the European powers, the United States – expected it to last a few weeks. In fact it took over two years for the best of Britain's regiments, almost half a million men altogether, to subdue the rough-and-ready burgher commandos of the Transvaal and Orange Free State.

The Boers had very much the upper hand during the first month or two, notching up resounding victories at Colenso, Stormberg and Magersfontein within the space of a few days, a period that became known to the Imperial forces as 'British Black Week'. They went on to besiege the key garrison towns of Mafeking, Kimberley and Ladysmith; on the eastern flank, the brilliant young general Louis Botha rolled up the railway line deep into Natal. But numbers, and greater resources, were eventually to tell. Redvers Buller finally managed to breach the Tugela line, relieving Ladysmith on 28 February, 1900. Lord Roberts and his chief-of-staff Horatio Kitchener pushed through the central front, occupying Johannesburg in May and Pretoria in June of the same year. It all seemed to be over bar the mopping up.

But the war was to drag on for another 23 long months, to cost tens of thousands of lives, and to devastate the northern territories. Boer commandos under such enterprising leaders as Botha, Christiaan de Wet, Jan Smuts and J.B.M. Hertzog took to the open veld, adopted hit-and-run tactics, and struck repeatedly at the enemy's communications, supplies and outlying garrisons. Against this rapier Kitchener (who was now in command) used the broadsword of blockhouse (over 8 000 of them) and barbed wire, scorched earth and concentration camp. Thirty thousand farmsteads were destroyed, whole villages burnt to the ground. Deneys Reitz, Boer soldier and son of a former Free State president, described a 'driven' area he passed through, 'leaving behind only blackened ruins and trampled fields, so that our course lay through a silent, unpeopled waste, across which we navigated our wagon like a lonely ship at sea'.

The women and children and the black labourers of the Boer farming areas were rounded up in their thousands and incarcerated in camps that were designed to intern, not to exterminate. Nevertheless, over 27 000 whites (including 22 000 children) and an unknown number of blacks died, mainly of disease, which spread like bush-fires in the overcrowded, unhygienic conditions. The scorching of the land, and the concentration camps, left a legacy that was to haunt two generations of South Africans.

Finally, exhausted, the Boers in the field came to terms. On 15 May, 1902, at a convention in Vereeniging, their leaders decided to negotiate. On 31 May, after nine days of hard bargaining, the two sides signed the Peace of Vereeniging at Melrose House, Pretoria.

RECONSTRUCTION AND UNION

Curiously, it was the architect of war, Alfred, Lord Milner, who was to become chief engineer of South Africa's post-war recovery. His aims were to repair the ravaged land and resettle the denuded areas; to bring the mines back into operation; to create a customs union, and to consolidate the peace — in fact, to build a new nation. Economic recovery, he believed, would heal the wounds of war, win back the goodwill of Transvaler and Free Stater. He exercised extreme diplomacy in his dealings with bloody but unbowed Afrikanerdom, publicly praising the Boers' 'patriotism, their courage, their resourcefulness, their endurance, their dignity and self-restraint in victory and their stoicism in defeat'.

Behind these splendid and sincere words, though, lurked the old Milner: his brave new world was to be an Anglo-Saxon one. His schemes included the settlement of 10 000 English-speaking farmers on the Highveld 'within a twelve-month'; in government schools 'Dutch should be used to teach English and English everything else', and so on.

His handling of racial issues, too, could hardly be termed progressive. The Native Affairs Commission was almost entirely made up of English-speaking whites, who encouraged the creation of 'locations' for urban blacks and the separation of the races.

Milner's policy of Anglicization met strong resistance from the Afrikaners. The recovery programme, on the other hand, succeeded beyond the expectations of even the most optimistic. To help get the economic wheels turning again, Milner gathered around him a group of talented young Oxford graduates — lawyers, administrators, economists: men such as Patrick Duncan (later Governor-General of South Africa); Lionel Curtis, author of the crucial Selborne Memorandum; Philip Kerr (who was to become British Ambassador to Washington); Geoffrey Dawson, future editor of the Johannesburg Star and of The Times of London; and John Buchan (Lord Tweedsmuir), the famed novelist and later Governor-General of Canada. They became known as 'Milner's kindergarten', and contributed brilliantly to the process of reconstruction.

Central to this process were the gold mines which, at that time, were suffering from a critical shortage of labour. African workers, scattered by the winds of war, were slow to return from the outlying regions. Milner decided on indentured Chinese labour, and the first arrived on the Reef in 1904; over 60 000 followed, and the issue became highly controversial both in South Africa and Britain. By 1910 all had been repatriated — but they had served their purpose: the mines began generating wealth from mid-decade on. There was progress, too, in the other sectors: most of the Boers were back on their lands by the end of 1902; a railway line was constructed between Kimberley and the Witwatersrand; another linked the Natal and Orange River colony systems. A subcontinental customs union came into being in 1903.

Meanwhile, there was a great deal of activity on the political front. Het Volk, an Afrikaner organization led by ex-generals Botha and Smuts, started lobbying for second-language and other sectional rights in 1905. There was also the Orangia Unie Afrikaner party. In due course both groups opened their membership lists to English-speakers; each won a resounding victory in elections to the legislatures of the self-governing colonies of the Transvaal and Orange River, both of which had been constituted in 1907.

Wider concepts, however, were taking hold of men's imaginations: first, political federation; then unification. Jan Smuts summed up the vision: 'What we want,' he said, 'is a supreme national authority to give expression to the national will of South Africa, and the rest is really subordinate.'

Political leaders in three territories and the white electorates of all four were in fact strongly in favour of Union (Natal's politicians were not, but voters in the referendum of 1908 gave an overwhelming mandate to the unionists). A National Convention deliberated the issue between October 1908 and May 1909, and most of its recommendations were incorporated into the Act of Union of 1910. On 31 May of that year, the four colonies became one country, independent, with Dominion status on the not-too-distant horizon. The form of government — the Westminster system, comprising two parliamentary chambers (the Senate acting in a largely advisory capacity), a cabinet of ten, four provincial authorities with considerable local powers, and a Governor-General representing the Crown — was to remain virtually unchanged until South Africa became a republic in 1961.

Bechuanaland, Basutoland and Swaziland were not part of the new political arrangement. They would remain within the British fold as High Commission territories until attaining full independence in the 1960s.

Significantly, blacks were excluded from the democratic process: they were to be represented by nominated whites. Only the Cape leadership had pushed, and pushed strenuously, for what was called a 'civilization test' (property, income, education) which would enfranchise some blacks and disenfranchise some whites. But the most that liberal-minded men such as W.P. Schreiner, the enlightened Afrikaner François Malan and Premier J.X. Merriman could achieve was reluctant agreement to constitutional entrenchment of the 'coloured vote' in the Cape and the right of mixed-descent people to seek election to the Cape Provincial Council. They received lukewarm support from Natal's traditionally moderate spokesmen and from the British Liberal Ministers, and strong opposition from the powerful northern politicians.

Also significant was the equal status accorded, within the constitution, to the Dutch and English languages. This was a major victory for those Afrikaners who had fought long and hard for all that it represented — Afrikaner identity and the emergence of Afrikanerdom as a coherent national political force.

GROWTH, CHANGE AND POLARIZATION

The years between Union in 1910 and the crucial parliamentary election of 1948 witnessed South Africa's transition from an uneven patchwork of colonial territories to a powerful modern industrial nation. They were also years of war, of profound social change, and of complex political interaction, probably better summarized by broad theme than in chronological sequence:

The political arena was dominated, throughout the entire span, by three Afrikaners, each of whom had served as a skilled military commander during the Anglo-Boer War.

Louis Botha held the Union premiership until his death in 1919, when the reins passed to Jan Smuts, his close associate and natural successor. Both were statesmen rather than politicians, both believed in conciliation between the two white cultural groups in South Africa; both were 'Empire men' in the sense that they valued close links with the former colonial power, each leading the country to war against Germany in support of Britain.

The third general, J.B.M. (Barry) Hertzog, was cast in an entirely different mould: a passionate nationalist, determined to entrench Afrikaner power, though towards the end of his political career he was obliged to compromise in the interests of political expediency.

Throughout the tortuous political manoeuvrings of the 1920s and 1930s Smuts and Hertzog occupied centre stage, most of the time in direct opposition to each other but actually coming together in 1933, during the depths of the Great Depression, to form a coalition cabinet with Hertzog as Prime Minister. At the end of the following year their former parties were fused under the umbrella of the United Party and the two leaders directed the affairs of an increasingly prosperous country until the outbreak of the Second World War in September 1939. At this point Hertzog, anti-British to the last, resigned.

Some Afrikaner nationalists, the hardline conservatives, had refused to follow Hertzog's lead in 1934. Instead, they formed their own 'Purified' National Party under the leadership of Cape clergyman and newspaper editor D.F. Malan. Smuts, preoccupied with world events during the war and in the years immediately afterwards, badly underestimated the grass roots appeal — among voters of both language groups — of a movement whose doctrinal corner-stone was apartheid, and at the 1948 general election his United Party paid the price.

The years of war. Twice during the twentieth century South African troops took to the battlefield in support of the country's western allies.

Before marching into German South-West Africa in 1915, Prime Minister Louis Botha was obliged to quell a full-scale insurrection at home. Memories of the concentration camps and the burning farms were still bitter among many Afrikaners: little more than a decade before, their men had been fighting for survival in their own valleys and veld, and now they were being asked to join 'the enemy' in a wider struggle. Altogether, some 11 000 burghers, led by Christiaan de Wet and other former guerilla heroes, rose against their government in the traditional Boer 'armed protest'; one large commando, situated near the then South-West African border, defected to the Germans.

But the rebels enjoyed too little support in the country as a whole, and the uprising was short-lived: by the beginning of 1915 they had been scattered by disciplined government troops; most of their leaders were arrested and imprisoned; one had drowned in the Vaal River and another was condemned and executed.

Botha could now turn his attention to the real enemy. He personally led a 12 000-man force from Swakopmund, Smuts another from Lüderitzbucht on the western coast; other columns marched in from the Orange River. The terrain was vast, and hostile, but the German occupying garrison small, and by mid-July it was all over. Observed *The Times* of London: 'To the youngest of the sister nations belongs the glory of the first complete triumph of our arms and the disappearance of Germany from the map of Africa.'

In the long run, though, the new occupation scarcely proved a blessing, certainly not to the international community. Administered by South Africa as a mandate of the League of Nations since 1920, renamed Namibia by the United Nations in 1968, it has been a source of constant diplomatic dispute.

Other South African theatres of operation in the First World War were East Africa and the European Western Front. In both, the Union forces fought with distinction. Smuts, appointed commander-in-chief of the Imperial Army in Africa, executed a long and ultimately successful campaign in the east against the elusive German general Paul Emil von Lettow-Vorbeck. Bloodier by far were the battles in Flanders' fields. In one, at Delville Wood in July 1916, 121 officers and 3 032 men of the South African Brigade held their positions against massive bombardment and counter-attack for almost a week, the unwounded survivors numbering just five officers and 750 men.

Once again, in 1939, there was controversy over South Africa's obligations. But Jan Smuts — soldier, statesman, scholar, friend of Winston Churchill and of Mohandas Gandhi, member of the Imperial War Cabinet and loyalist (he was one of the prime architects of the Statute of Westminster which, in 1931, proclaimed the Commonwealth of Nations) — carried the parliamentary vote by 80 to 67. Opposition continued throughout the war, its active instrument the underground *Ossewabrandwag*. Generally speaking, though, the opponents of involvement were very much in the minority; whites of both language groups volunteered for active service in large numbers, as did those of mixed descent. South African troops joined battle with Nazi Germany and its allies, again in East Africa (inflicting a stunning defeat on Mussolini's Italian forces in Abyssinia), in the Western Desert and in Europe, slogging their way up the spine of Italy in one of the hardest and most thankless campaigns of the war.

Economic growth. Exploitation of the Witwatersrand gold-fields triggered the move, from the early years of the twentieth century, towards industrialization, and by definition urbanization — developments that changed the face of South Africa. Primary industry created the base for an impressive superstructure of heavy secondary industries, most notable of the early ones being ISCOR, the massive State-controlled corporation which processes local iron and coal reserves to produce (and export) steel. ISCOR came on stream in 1934. The mining industry has expanded steadily

POLITICS AND PROTEST. The years following the National Party's victory at the 1948 polls brought Draconian social regulation, the formal entrenchment of 'apartheid' (later called Separate Development) and a widening racial divide. White liberal opposition, largely English-speaking, became increasingly ineffectual.

British Royalty visited South Africa for the last time in 1947 (1). The new regime (2): Prime Minister D.F. Malan (holding hat) flanked by, from left, C.R. Swart, Minister of Justice for the initial eleven, critical, years of Nationalist rule and who later served as the Republic's first State President; N.C. Havenga, Minister of Finance from 1948 to 1955; J.G. Strijdom, who succeeded Malan as premier; and Dr E.G. Jansen. The personification of South Africa's industrial and financial enterprise: Sir Ernest Oppenheimer (3), whose family has been a powerful force on the side of moderation. Extra-parliamentary political activity in the 1950s included mass rallies by the Torch Commando (4), a movement formed to protest

NATIVE LAWS AMENDMENT BILL
THIS SOUNDS THE DEATH KNELL FOR SOUTH AFRICA UNLESS YOU OPPOSE !

WYSIGINGSWETSONTWERP OP ATURELLEWETGEWING
DIT BETEKEN DIE DOODSKLOK VIR SUID-AFRIKA TENSY U DAARTEEN VERSET !

8

9

the new race laws, and silent vigils by the women of the Black Sash (5). Leader of the Parliamentary Opposition during this period was Sir De Villiers Graaf (6), who presided over the slow demise of Smuts's once-mighty United Party. Hendrik Verwoerd (7), doyen of the social engineers and Prime Minister from 1958 until his assassination in September 1966. Nobel Peace Prize-winner Albert Luthuli (8), the non-violent voice of Black aspiration, with visiting US Senator Robert Kennedy. Alan Paton (9), author of *Cry, the Beloved Country*. For almost a century the 'mail boats' (10) provided the physical link and symbolized the traditional loyalties between Britain and South Africa. The last of the great ships, *Windsor Castle*, sailed out of Table Bay on 6 September 1977. The watershed tragedy: burial of the victims of police action at Sharpeville, 1960 (11). Until then, despite mounting criticism, South Africa had been regarded as a full member of the international community; afterwards, the country receded ever further into isolation.

throughout the century (*see* page 44), providing a solid base for the increasingly sophisticated manufacturing sector. Two global wars and a world greedy for South Africa's raw materials and processed goods reinforced the impetus.

At the same time periodic drought, depression and new, labour-efficient farming techniques were forcing small farmers and tenant *bywoners* (squatters) off the land and into the cities in droves. The 'poor white' problem was first identified as early as 1890; the Transvaal Indigency Commission reported a few years later that tens of thousands of refugees from the country areas were living 'in wretched shanties on the outskirts of towns', where they competed – largely unsuccessfully – with low-earning black labour being drawn into the industrial system. In 1931 a Carnegie Corporation-funded investigation revealed that, of a white South African population of some 1,8 million, more than 300 000 had to be classed as 'very poor'.

This was of course at the depth of the Great Depression, and things would get better. Large-scale government assistance schemes, increasing prosperity, the organized training of skills and the growing manufacturing sector absorbed more and more white labour, and by the end of the 1930s, according to one historian, 'the poor white problem had virtually ceased to exist'. It did, however, leave a painful legacy, especially within official labour policy: the State would borrow from socialism to become the major employer, and job reservation would impose its artificial controls until the 1970s.

South Africa's labour relations story is not an especially happy one. Strikes and unrest were a depressingly regular feature of the industrial scene throughout the decades after Union. Most convulsive was the so-called 'Red Revolt' in 1922. In January of that year 22 000 Rand miners and engineering and power-station workers went on strike and organized themselves into paramilitary commandos, which were soon enough infiltrated by Marxist activists bent on a workers' revolution. Pitched battles broke out; troops were mobilized; 153 people (including 72 of the State forces) were killed, 534 wounded.

This particular upheaval gave graphic point to one of the constants in the social and economic history of modern South Africa: white fear of black encroachment. Times were hard in the 1920s and '30s; black labour extremely cheap (miners earned 2s.2d. a day). It was publicly estimated that if 50 per cent of the white labour force could be replaced by blacks the mines would save £1 million a year (a huge amount in those days). Mine managements knew the facts; so did the unions, and the barricades went up as soon as it was announced, in December 1921, that 2 000 semi-skilled white gold-miners would be declared redundant.

Black urbanization, naturally, ran parallel to white. A new proletariat, officially regarded as 'temporary' and composed in part of tens of thousands of migrants from adjacent territories, collected in the enormous, controlled townships that began to mushroom around the mining and industrial centres of the Reef, Natal and the eastern Cape from the first years of the century. Black security of tenure and the right to collective industrial action were two of the major reforms introduced in the early 1980s.

THE SOCIAL ENGINEERS

The National Party which formed a government – with a slim parliamentary majority of five – under the premiership of Dr D.F. Malan in 1948 has remained in power for almost 40 years, though its composition and some of its ideological tenets have undergone radical change.

During the first two decades the formal division, or stratification, along racial lines provided the thrust of policy. Separate development (later to be called multi-national development) was seen to be the solution to the immense problems of cultural diversity and conflicting group interests. Linchpin of a Draconian and wide-ranging legislative programme was the Group Areas Act of 1950, which segregated, among other things, the country's residential areas. Further statutes included those involving freedom of movement, indentity documents, the formal classification of people according to colour, regulation of workplace and a vast arsenal of security laws.

All this was not entirely new: the ingredients of the southern African melting pot had never really melted. They were kept apart, from the early colonial days, by competition, by perhaps irreconcilable cultural distinctions, by fierce informal pressures and by formal edict. In the words of eminent historian T.R.H. Davenport, the Native (Urban Areas) Act of 1923, for example, 'grew into one of the most complex pieces of control legislation ever devised anywhere' – before the Nationalists took control. Other precedents abound. But from 1949 there were both qualitative and quantitative differences. Now, for the first time, Afrikanerdom was in the national driving seat, and for the first time rigid segregation was entrenched within an all-embracing legal code and structured administration.

There were laws, too, affecting the coloured people. In 1951 the Separate Registration of Voters Act, designed to remove coloured voters from the common roll (they were to be represented in Parliament by four white Members) was passed but subsequently declared invalid by the Appellate Division of the Supreme Court. Five controversial years later, however, and after a startling series of constitutional acrobatics, the Act became effective. In 1969 the last vestiges of coloured parliamentary representation ended, to be replaced by the partly-elected, partly-nominated Coloured Persons Representative Council (CRC).

But it was the status and future of the black people that preoccupied the Nationalist government. Under Malan and his successors – J.G. Strijdom (1954-1958) and, especially, Hendrik Verwoerd (1958-1966) – the policy of enforced segregation was carried to its logical extremes.

In its simplest form, the argument held that the blacks had their own, traditional territories and that it was in these that they should exercise the legitimate rights of citizenship and the vote. The long, laborious process of creating separate black states began in a modest way with the Black Authorities Act of 1951 (it set up tribal, regional and territorial authorities *within* the Union of South Africa), and reached its legislative zenith in 1959 with the Promotion of Black Self-Government Act. This provided for the establishment of homelands (later known as national states) for the country's main black groups, and for the development in these territories of governmental institutions which would eventually lead, in each case and by predetermined stages, to full independence. These stages are:

☐ *First*: partial self-government (legislative assembly; executive council; chief minister; revenue fund; public service commission; but no High Court).

☐ *Second*: self-governing status within the Republic of South Africa (legislative assembly; cabinet; High Court; flag and national anthem).

☐ *Third*: at any time the national state may request the Republic for full and untrammelled independence.

Four have done so. Transkei became independent in 1976, Bophuthatswana in 1977, Venda in 1979 and Ciskei in 1981 (*see* page 14). The remaining six, at the time of writing, are at the second stage. They are Lebowa, Gazankulu, Qwaqwa, KwaZulu, KaNgwane and KwaNdebele.

KwaZulu, with its four million Nguni and proud history, has chosen not to take the route of full independence, as Chief Minister Buthelezi regards his people as South Africans, opposes the fragmentation of the country into tight little compartments, and urges an integrated (though not necessarily a unitary) system. He also includes among the preliminary options the fusion of black KwaZulu and Asian and white Natal to form a single political entity.

THE REPUBLIC

Significantly, D.F. Malan, just before he assumed office, supported the granting to India of a republican constitution within the Commonwealth. The Nationalists, chafed by the tenuous but irritating Imperial bonds that were the legacy of Union and Dominion status, aspired to the same freedom, and the issue was openly broached by Hendrik Verwoerd in the early months of 1960 (British premier Harold MacMillan's 'wind of change' address to the joint Houses of Parliament in Cape Town reinforced an already strong resolve to cut the ties). A referendum was held later in the year at which the electorate, by a majority of 74 580 votes (1 626 336 were cast), decided in favour of a republican form of government.

In the interim serious unrest had broken out in parts of the country, the culmination of sporadic riots that had started the year before in protest against the enforced carrying of reference books (passes) and largely orchestrated by the Pan-Africanist Congress (see page 34). On 21 March, 1960 police confronted a large crowd in the township of Sharpeville, near Vereeniging in the Transvaal; shots were fired; 69 blacks were killed and numbers wounded. There were also riots and, soon afterwards, massive protest marches in Cape Town. The PAC and its big brother the African National Congress were banned. A state of emergency was declared.

Sharpeville was a seminal event. Before the shooting the country, for all the criticism levelled at it, was accepted as a member of the international community; after March 1960 it faced increasing isolation. Exactly a year later Verwoerd flew to London to apply for continued Commonwealth membership of a republican South Africa. Harsh words were exchanged at the conference; South Africa withdrew its application, and two months later the Republic was formally established.

Hendrik Verwoerd, Holland-born and Rhodesian-educated, doctrinaire, brilliant, ruthless and uncompromising, died on 6 September, 1966 — victim of an assassin's knife (the killer was a parliamentary messenger, subsequently adjudged unfit to stand trial). Verwoerd had been the chief architect of separate development, designing and constructing a monolithic structure that would become the increasingly sharp focus of critical attention, both inside South Africa and internationally. It would also present his successors with possibly the toughest of political, and moral, challenges.

DIALOGUE AND PROTEST

The man who succeeded Verwoerd, B.J. Vorster, was also a hard-line conservative, but a pragmatic one who perceived the dangerous long-term consequences of isolation and the need to establish 'normal and friendly relations' with African states (in fact Verwoerd had also recognized the realities, but too late to translate conviction into effective action). The Republic was an African country, the most powerful south of the Sahara; some states were economically dependent on it; the whole complex of southern African nations economically interdependent.

This was the era of détente and dialogue, and a significant degree of rapprochement, or at least of contact, was achieved. A flurry of diplomatic activity in the late 1960s and 1970s produced some positive results: Malawi established formal links with Pretoria; closer ties were forged with Lesotho, Botswana and Swaziland; the South African premier paid successful goodwill visits to Malawi (1969); the Ivory Coast (1974) and Liberia (1975). There were reciprocal courtesies: Vorster met Zambia's Kenneth Kaunda at the Victoria Falls in 1975 in a joint effort to solve the thorny problem of Rhodesia's rebellion (the country had unilaterally declared its independence from Britain in November 1965, an act which polarized racial opinion and inhibited the whole détente exercise). In the end it was Vorster who, with Henry Kissinger, the United States Secretary of State, was instrumental in bringing Rhodesian leader Ian Smith to the negotiating table.

Farther afield, however, the story was by no means one of unqualified success. On the contrary, South Africa's relations with the international community, with countries beyond her immediate sphere of influence, continued to deteriorate. Criticism of the Republic's internal arrangements mounted at the United Nations; the Carter Administration's Andrew Young stirred the hitherto distracted American liberal conscience; a militarily successful but diplomatically disastrous incursion into Marxist Angola (responsibility was as much Washington's as Pretoria's) helped fix the international spotlight on what was seen as a 'destabilization' policy and on the intractable question of Namibian independence.

Nor was all quiet on the home front. In June 1976 unrest erupted in the sprawling township of Soweto (in fact Soweto is a city of well over a million black residents) near Johannesburg and spread to other centres, continuing in varying degrees of intensity for almost eight months. The subsequent commission of inquiry found that the immediate cause was the use of Afrikaans as a teaching medium in black high schools. General discrimination, lack of citizenship, restrictions on property ownership and lack of civic facilities were powerful contributory factors. The riots, however, were not spontaneous incidents but rather part of a sustained, organized campaign, launched by a number of black consciousness organizations, to undermine the social order. In October 1977 the Government banned 18 of these bodies together with many of their leaders (see page 34).

Education in fact has been one of the basic issues underlying grass roots protest over the years. To digress for a moment:

In South Africa, schooling is largely separate and unequal: the average black primary classroom has 50 pupils; there is a critical shortage of qualified teachers; the drop-out rate is alarming: in 1984, nearly 18 per cent of the total number of black school-going children was in the first year of school and only 1,7 per cent in the final year.

By contrast there is compulsory education, up to the age of 16, for whites, and relatively easy access to universities and other tertiary institutions.

The inequalities are recognized, and there have been a few modest moves towards remedying the imbalance, but in the long run it all comes down to the depressing realities of Third World socio-economics. The ideal is a non-discriminatory system that permits universal compulsory education of a high standard. The cake, though, is simply not large enough. The essential choice would therefore seem to be between, on the one hand, spreading the country's very limited education resources across the board to provide inadequate schooling for all and, on the other hand, perpetuating the élitist approach but in a somewhat different guise. The latter option would almost certainly give the independent, privately funded or fee-paying non-racial school a new and striking prominence on the South African canvas.

OPPOSING FORCES

The origin of the South African extra-parliamentary opposition movements – if one discounts the lone voices of late nineteenth century black intellectuals such as Tiyo Soga and John Tengo Jabavu – are properly to be found in the years of disenchantment that followed the Anglo-Boer War. British 'non-racial justice', anticipated when the two northern territories returned to colonial rule, simply did not materialize, and a number of black congress-type associations made their appearance in the four British colonies (the Vigilance Association in the eastern Cape/Transkei; the SA Native Congress in the western Cape; the Natal Native Congress, and the Transvaal Congress). They were vocal enough, but ineffective.

Nor did blacks have a say in the deliberations that created the Union of South Africa in 1910 (see page 28). Despite strenuous representations to the British constitution-makers, the future was shaped without consultation with blacks. A Durban lawyer, Dr Pixley Seme, became the moving spirit in the launching of the South African Native National Congress in 1912 – a body later (in 1925) renamed the African National Congress.

At about the same time, a talented Indian advocate was crusading, successfully, for Asian rights in South Africa. Mohandas K. Gandhi had arrived in Durban in 1893 to take up a private legal brief; he founded the Natal Indian Congress a year later and, during two decades of political confrontation (he was imprisoned twice) finally reached an accord with General Jan Smuts. It was during these years that Gandhi evolved his political philosophy and technique, *satyagraha* – commonly termed passive resistance but more literally 'keeping to the truth'. He returned to India in 1914 to work long, hard and ultimately triumphantly for that country's independence.

The history of the black opposition movement – that is to say, of the African National Congress in particular, although labour and church organizations were active and articulate in the between-war years – is a complicated narrative, most neatly encapsulated perhaps by Professor T. Kasis: 'Successively, the ANC retained liberal expectations, became more militant, attempted passive resistance, entered a multiracial popular front, was overtaken by impatient black nationalism, and moved underground.'

The passive resistance phase came to an abrupt end with the enactment of the Criminal Law Amendment Bill in 1952. ANC president at the time was Chief Albert Luthuli, a Rhodesian-born Zulu aristocrat and churchman. He was formally 'banned' in 1952 but his moral leadership – he advocated universal suffrage but renounced violence – continued to be acknowledged by the majority of members. Luthuli was awarded the Nobel Peace Prize in 1961.

After 1952 the ANC, for a time, operated within a loose, non-racial confederation known as the Congress Alliance whose ideological platform became the Freedom Charter, a code adopted and signed at a rally in Kliptown in 1955. Other signatories were the SA Coloured People's Organisation, various Indian congresses and the white Congress of Democrats.

The Freedom Charter is the key to any understanding of the immensely intricate political scene in modern South Africa. The signatories and their ideological successors subscribe to a non-racial solution to the country's problems. On the other side of a fundamental divide are those who eschew the Charter, seeking an exclusively black, Marxist-socialist solution. This lies at the root of much of the black-on-black violence of the mid-1980s.

The more militant, mainly younger elements of the ANC, those who walked the black-only path, broke away from the parent body in 1959 to form the Pan-Africanist Congress. A year later

Sharpeville brought the rivalry into sharp focus: each organization campaigned vigorously against the pass laws, urging township blacks to leave their reference (pass) books at home, invite arrest, overload the entire security system. On 28 March, 1960 both the ANC and the PAC were banned in terms of the Unlawful Organisations Act, and went underground, and into exile. The ANC formed its military wing, *Umkonto we Sizwe* ('spear of the nation'): its targets were 'hard' objectives: government installations, communications and so forth. Loss of life was to be avoided. Poqo, the PAC's counterpart, had more murderous intent.

The sabotage campaign was waged intensively until the mid-1960s. There were arrests; some of the leaders, including Oliver Tambo, went into exile; the ANC split once again, the radical communist element departing, leaving Tambo and his nationalists in control. The communist purge, though, was to be short-lived. One of the most influential presences later to emerge on the ANC power base, for instance, was Joe Slovo, a white member of the South African Communist Party (banned in 1950).

Some, like Nelson Mandela, the ANC's president, did not go into exile. At the Rivonia Trial in 1964 Mandela and a number of other Congress figures, including Walter Sisulu and Dennis Goldberg, were charged under the General Law Amendment Act (the 'Sabotage Act') and the Suppression of Communism Act and sentenced to life imprisonment.

The arena, from the late 1960s and especially in the 1970s, became even more crowded. 'Black consciousness' organizations, led by the younger breed, appeared on the scene. In 1977 a full 18 bodies were banned, their leaders detained – including Steve Biko, who died in custody in controversial circumstances. The fragmentation of the black opposition movement, though, continued as follows:

☐ The Azanian People's Organisation (Azapo), which does not subscribe to the Freedom Charter, was formed in 1979. It was followed by two youthful bodies which do endorse the Charter's non-racial principles:

☐ The Azanian Students Organisation (Azaso), and:

☐ The Congress of South African Students (Cosas).

☐ Less radical and more specific in its aims was the Committee of Ten of Soweto, led by Dr Nthato Motlana and established to oppose the system of appointed local-government committees.

☐ Two powerful umbrella organizations were inaugurated in the early 1980s. The United Democratic Front, an alliance of over 400 civic, church, sports and trade union bodies and claiming to represent a million people and more, was launched in August 1983 at Mitchell's Plain, a coloured town in the western Cape, specifically to oppose the government's proposed new tricameral constitutional dispensation (see page 39). Its patrons included the Rev. Alan Boesak, president of the World Alliance of Churches; Nelson Mandela; Dr Beyers Naudé; and Helen Joseph and Hassan Howa of the South African Council of Sport. The UDF subscribes to the Freedom Charter.

☐ Also founded in 1983 was the exclusively black National Forum Committee, the second umbrella organization, which included Azapo in its membership and adopted, as a kind of counterpoint to the Charter, a 'Manifesto of the Azanian People'. It described the central political issue as 'a racial class struggle' in which all whites featured as 'capitalists' and blacks as 'workers'.

☐ Two other personalities to emerge as strong leaders of current black opinion were Nobel Prize winner Bishop Desmond Tutu, and Chief Mangosuthu Buthelezi, Chief Minister of KwaZulu and head of the powerful Inkatha organization.

While these associations worked within the legal framework, the African National Congress remained banned, its titular head, Nelson Mandela, imprisoned. The violence of the mid-1980s can thus be divided into three categories:

First, the continuation of the ANC's campaign of sabotage aimed, as before, at the inanimate rather than the animate, though by mid-decade there were ominous signs that straightforward terror tactics would replace the selective approach. Its operations were severely inhibited by the Nkomati Accord, signed by South Africa and Mozambique in March 1984, and by reciprocal agreements with the governments of Swaziland, Botswana and Lesotho.

Second, sustained mob unrest directed at established authority, its sympathizers and at property, which was designed to 'render the country ungovernable'.

Third, inter-faction murder and mayhem, much of it representing the struggle between those who endorsed the Freedom Charter and those who did not; some of it of a vigilante nature. Speculation about a sinister conservative 'third force' remained unsubstantiated.

A state of emergency, covering 36 magisterial districts (out of 260) was declared in 1985. In October that year it was lifted in a number of areas and extended to others, including the hitherto unaffected western Cape.

In March 1986 the state of emergency was lifted altogether: a widely welcomed move, though in some critical quarters enthusiasm was tempered by apprehension about possible moves to confer wider powers on the South African Police to deal with local unrest situations.

The emergency cost the country dearly: in terms of adverse international publicity and the consequent loss of investor confidence, and above all in terms of human life.

P.W. BOTHA AND THE PACE OF REFORM

The National Party celebrated its thirtieth year in office in 1978 — three decades during which separation had been sedulously entrenched and which saw South Africa elevated to the higher ranks of industrial nations.

That year, though, was to mark the start of a new era. In September B.J. Vorster resigned to become State President, and was replaced by former Minister of Defence P.W. Botha. These changes took place in the middle of what became known as the Information Scandal. Probes by Press, police and, later, the Erasmus Commission revealed that government funds had been misused by officials in the Department of Information, and that the Prime Minister of the time had known of the irregularities. Vorster resigned the presidency. Also implicated was Dr Connie Mulder, former Minister of Information, who resigned his seat in the House.

The new premier made it clear from the outset that he was determined on a reformist course. The Information controversy delayed the initiative for almost a year, but in August 1979 Botha outlined a 12-point plan to the Natal congress of the National Party: his 'total strategy' for the security and gradual transformation of the social and political order. The plan included provision for power devolution, the recognition of the rights of ethnic groups, the consolidation of national states, the creation of a 'constellation of southern African states', the removal of 'unnecessary discrimination', and, above all, a new constitutional dispensation (see below).

The economic climate was right for change. Never had South Africa seemed so prosperous; new political structures would require massive finance, and in the late 1970s and early 1980s wealth was being generated at an unprecedented rate. The gold price had sky-rocketed, topping $800 an ounce at one point; in 1980 the economy registered an eight per cent growth rate; annual per capita income reached R2 000, a phenomenal ten times more than in 1960; foreign trade totalled R34 000 million, placing South Africa fifteenth in the hierarchy of the world's trading nations; foreign investment amounted to R25 000 million.

The most dramatic moves were on the labour front. Two commissions of inquiry, the Wiehahn and the Riekert, had together recommended the maximum use of all available skills and the removal of almost every law that discriminated against black workers. Government accepted most of the recommendations.

Job reservation along racial lines had long been subject to natural erosion, the artificial barriers crumbling under the pressure of market forces. Now, with the active participation of the private sector, blacks were to be brought fully into the body economic through intensified training, integration and the elimination of the wage gap. Collective bargaining, in fact, was to prove one of the keys to genuine advancement. Black trade unions, fully recognized, would be the sharpest instrument in the operation to improve the lot of the urban black. In the event, the unions organized themselves with remarkable speed and expertise, giving the black workforce powerful economic and, potentially, political muscle almost overnight.

In due course, other significant changes occurred in the urban context: black townsfolk achieved a more permanent status with the right to purchase homes on long (99-year) lease and later, in many instances, to buy houses outright even though they were technically citizens of national states rather than of the Republic of South Africa. (Dual citizenship is, at the time of writing, a prospect receiving increasing attention.) Above all, influx control and the 'pass laws' were finally legislated out of existence in 1986, and a new and far less provocative system of identity documentation introduced.

However, the thrust of the Botha strategy was — had to be — in the constitutional field. The Senate was abolished in 1980, signalling the demise of the Westminster system in South Africa. A new body, the President's Council, comprising 60 nominated coloured, Indian and white members, was established to investigate and recommend a new constitution. This it did, presenting its package in May 1982.

The recommendations, which were accepted, made provision for an Executive President, a Parliament of three Houses (white, Asian and coloured), a non-racial Cabinet; a reconstituted President's Council and changes, intended to accommodate some black political aspirations, at local and regional government level (see page 40).

Prime Minister Botha announced that the proposals would be put to the test of a referendum to be held on 2 November, 1983.

The Labour Party, a major voice of the coloured people and long an opponent of the established government, joined the official Indian bodies in endorsing the plan. So too did the white New Republic Party, rump of the old United Party. Ranged against the dispensation were parties to the left — the Progressive Federal Party under the leadership at the time of Dr Frederick van Zyl Slabbert — and to the right: the Conservative Party and the Herstigte Nasionale Party.

The Conservative leader, Dr Andries Treurnicht, had resigned his Cabinet portfolio in 1982 and, together with ex-Ministers Connie Mulder and Ferdinand Hartzenberg, had formed the party to fight what was perceived as a dangerous 'drift to the left'. Sixteen right-wing MPs joined the new organization, whose power-base lay largely in the north of the country.

A strong but voteless voice opposing the proposed tricameral system was that of KwaZulu's Chief Buthelezi. The black political organizations mentioned on page 34 also condemned the propo-

CRACKS IN THE EDIFICE. The two decades since the assassination of Prime Minister H.F. Verwoerd (1), brought intensifying pressures against South Africa's political and social structures from both within and without. Verwoerd was succeeded by the hard-line but pragmatic B.J. Vorster, who in turn relinquished office, in controversial circumstances, to P.W. Botha, a reformist whose constitutional initiatives divided both the National Party and the country.

1976 was a watershed year: on 16 June students took to the streets in a frenzy of violence (2) directed primarily against inequalities in education, though the roots of discontent went deeper. Vorster, flanked by Cabinet colleagues, speaks of the need for detente (3). His 'outward-looking policy' had some measure of success. Its high point was his rôle in bringing Rhodesian rebel premier Ian Smith (4) to the negotiating table. Dr. Connie Mulder (5), one of the lead-

6

9

7

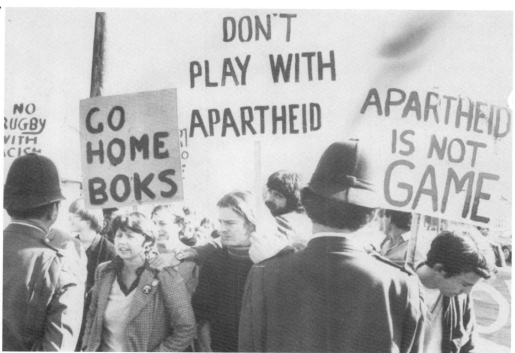

NO RUGBY WITH RACISM

GO HOME BOKS

DON'T PLAY WITH APARTHEID

APARTHEID IS NOT GAME

10

ers of the National Party's right wing, resigned his ministerial portfolio and his Party membership in 1978, and later helped form the opposition Conservative Party. The new Prime Minister, P.W. Botha **(6)**, with Kwa-Zulu's Chief Mangosuthu Buthelezi, (*left*) and Venda's Chief Patrick Mphephu. Black participation in decision-making at the highest political level is the central issue in South Africa today. Massive demonstrations in New Zealand against apartheid **(7)** threatened to disrupt the Springbok rugby tour in 1981. Botha launched his reformist campaign in the 1980s with the inauguration of the tricameral constitutional arrangement, which brought the Coloured and Indian peoples into the body politic. Pictured **(8)** is the Rev. Alan Hendrickse, leader of the majority Labour Party in the House of Representatives. Widespread township violence again erupted in 1985 **(9)**. Former leader of the liberal Progressive Federal Party and of the official Opposition, Dr. F. Van Zyl Slabbert **(10)**, resigned his parliamentary seat in 1986, claiming that Parliament was no longer an effective agent of basic reform.

8

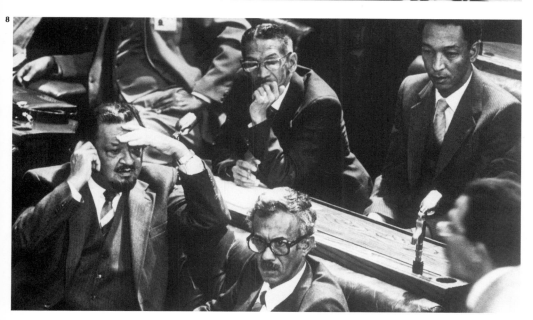

sals. So, too, did the United Democratic Front, who lobbied intensively for a 'no' response.

In the event, the white electorate gave overwhelming approval to the new constitution: 66 per cent voted in favour — a signal victory for P.W. Botha and a rare demonstration of Afrikaans- and English-speaking unity.

The process of reform got under way during the first session of the new Parliament. High points were the abolition of the Mixed Marriages Act and Section 16 of the Immorality Act. The real significance, though, was that whites and people of colour were for the first time deliberating and legislating together, that change was very much in the air; that the dyke had been breached and the trickle of reform would eventually, become a flood.

Coincident with all this was a sudden and deep economic recession, triggered originally by unfavourable commodity markets, a falling gold price and State over-spending; latterly by unrest, serious inflation, loss of banking and investor confidence and a declining rand exchange rate. Harsh Government measures taken in 1985 promised painful belt-tightening for an indeterminate but considerable period.

Ironically, or perhaps predictably, this was the time chosen by black opposition organizations and important sections of the international community to intensify pressure on the South African government. The disinvestment debate; sanctions; sporting isolation; township violence and the state of emergency occupied the headlines. The issue, for many, was not the reality of reform (or rather, the will to explore and institute reforms) but rather the nature of change, and how quickly it could and should be brought about, and whether this would involve power-sharing or power division.

SOUTH AFRICA TODAY

Southern Africa is a region in transition. President P.W. Botha's reform initiative, inaugurated with the establishment of a new constitutional dispensation early in 1984, prised open the first cracks in a monolithic governmental and administrative structure that had stood firm for three decades. The cracks widened as the initiative was taken forward, beckoned by common sense and conscience but also pushed, and pushed hard, by internal disturbance and external pressure. The situation is likely to remain fluid for some time to come.

The brief outline that follows reflects the position at the time of going to press. Some of the specifics are likely to be subject to modification, even to radical change, in the months to come.

GOVERNMENT

In September 1984 South Africa abandoned the Westminster system of government established by the Act of Union in 1910 and adopted a complex new constitution. This was designed to give the Asian and coloured people formal, though qualified, representation at the highest level. Blacks were not so represented: the issues of citizenship and the vote for black people were constitutionally and directly linked to the arrangement of self-governing and national states (*see* overleaf and pages 14 and 32).

Principal ingredients of the constitution are an executive president; a three-chamber parliament; the calculated division of governmental responsibilities into the classifications of 'national affairs' and 'own affairs'; a multiracial Cabinet; a Ministers' Council (equivalent to a Cabinet) for each of the three Houses of Parliament, and a largely consultative but influential President's Council. To elaborate:

□ The tricameral parliament comprises, first, the all-white House of Assembly of 178 members, 166 of whom are directly elected by white citizens of 18 years and over; four of whom are appointed on a provincial basis by the State President and the remaining eight elected by Members on a party-political basis.

Of the coloured people's 85-member House of Representatives, 80 members are directly elected by qualified voters (franchise qualifications for the three population groups are identical) – 66 of them from the Cape Province, where the great majority of mixed-descent citizens live. Five are 'special' members: two nominated by the State President and three elected by members on a party-political basis.

The Asian community's House of Delegates has 45 members, 29 of whom represent Natal constituents. Forty are directly elected; two are appointed; three are elected by sitting members.

The life of Parliament cannot extend beyond five years. The second general election under the new constitution will therefore be held, at the latest, in 1989.

□ The State President was, until 1984, a figurehead; now, in terms of the constitution, he has extensive executive powers. In matters of real substance, however, he acts in consultation with the Cabinet, of which he is chairman – a consensus approach to

government which is more implicit than explicit in the definition of his office.

The presidential term coincides with that of Parliament, the chief executive being elected to office at the end of each five-year period by a complicated voting system within the tricameral arrangement. The electoral college comprises 88 members: 50 from the House of Assembly, 25 from the House of Representatives, and 13 from the House of Delegates.

□ The overall executive structure is pyramidal. At the apex are the President and Cabinet who handle matters that affect all population groups – what are known as 'general affairs'. Matters that are deemed to be of sectional rather than common interest, however – those that are termed 'own affairs' – fall within the briefs of the separate Houses and their executive arms, the three Ministerial Councils. A member of a Ministers' Council must have his appointment approved by the appropriate House majority.

□ This separation is fundamental to the entire arrangement. To use official phraseology: 'For the first time in South Africa's constitutional history, each of the three population groups has full legislative and executive authority in its own affairs while assuming joint responsibility for all national affairs.' Within the latter category are portfolios covering such matters as defence, foreign relations, the national economy and internal security. In the former, the 'own affairs' classification, are welfare services, education, health, housing, community development, local government, agricultural services, water supplies, facilities for cultural and recreational activities, the electoral arrangements for group parliamentary representation and, finally, the finances and staffing relevant to the particular group's affairs.

□ The constitution is especially complex when it comes to legislation in the arena of national, or 'general', affairs. ('Own affairs' procedures are more straightforward, requiring the traditional Westminster-style cross-floor debate, three readings and majority approval.)

Consensus, as opposed to conflict, is the key objective in the national law-making process, a procedure designed to obtain across-the-board endorsement for new statutes. It depends for its success largely on the operation of the multiracial standing committees (that is, representatives drawn from all three chambers), which are appointed, as consultative bodies, for each ministerial portfolio. The mechanisms operate in this fashion:

– After the first reading – essentially the announcement of a bill – the proposal is referred straightaway to the appropriate standing committee for examination.

– The committee reports on the draft bill.

– The relevant Minister delivers his second-reading address to a plenary sitting of the three Houses.

– Each House debates the bill in detail.

– If the bill receives general approval, it is referred to the State President for his formal signature.

– If there is no consensus, or if substantial amendments are recommended, the bill may either be referred back to the standing committee for further scrutiny or go into an orthodox 'committee stage' (a special parliamentary committee is appointed), after which it will be given a third reading and, again, debated in each House.

– Should there still be no agreement, in spite of examination by Cabinet and joint standing committee, the proposed legislation is submitted to the President's Council (*see* below) for its recommendations.

– The President's council is principally an advisory body but has one, very important, function as arbitrator. It comprises 60 members, of whom 20 are appointed by majority vote in the House of Assembly, ten by the House of Representatives and five by the House of Delegates. The remaining 25 are nominated by the State President (ten of these, though, are designated proportionately by the opposition parties in the three Houses).

The Council advises the State President in any and all national matters (for instance, in 1985 it recommended the abolition of influx control) except draft legislation in process. It is in the latter realm, however, that it plays a crucial role. When the draft bill is held up – when, for example, the three Houses are in conflict and there are three substantially different versions – the Council can be asked for a decision. It will debate the issue and choose one of the versions (it may not amend, merely select). Its decision is then binding on all three Houses.

Alternatively, the Council may decide to confine its contribution to recommendations to the State President on ways in which the conflict can be resolved and consensus reached.

☐ The black people do not, at the time of writing, have a place in the parliamentary scheme, though black participation within the legislative system is under discussion. It has been held that the system of independent national states adequately accommodates their political aspirations. However, a great many black families, even though technically citizens of one or other national state, live permanently in the Republic of South Africa, the vast majority in and around the urban centres, and a degree of political representation – at local government and regional level – is being conferred.

The initial framework for black autonomy at local level was created by the Black Local Authorities Act of 1983, a measure intended to establish black municipalities identical in structure and function to those of the white urban communities.

Above this is the proposed 'second tier' of government, the Regional Services Councils, an attempt by government to restructure the administration of the country from grass roots level. These are multiracial bodies, made up of councillors nominated by each of the elected local authorities for each of the races within the designated region. Their revenue source is local taxation; central government subsidies are to be phased out. The councils will have undisputed authority in such matters as the administration of public transport, roads, water and electricity supplies, health services, infrastructural development, environmental conservation, tourism.

They will not, however, be equipped to administer many services directly but rather to act as a kind of 'wholesaler', providing bulk services to the individual municipalities.

Black people have therefore been granted a modicum of authority but as yet have no parliamentary voice within South Africa. This is the central issue of formal debate and less formal, often violent, opposition.

The process of reform continues, with Government seeking an accommodation through peaceful negotiation. The argument focuses, not on the principle of change – the huge majority of South Africans, black and white, agree on the need for and inevitability of change – but rather on its nature and pace. Intense inter-national lobbying and internal pressure have been a constant accompaniment of the debate.

In mid-1985 President Botha, in an address to the Natal Congress of the National Party (televised worldwide, a measure of the international preoccupation with South African affairs), and at subsequent congresses, reviewed the political scene in largely unspecific terms, but some crucial departures from traditional policy did emerge. These included affirmations that:

☐ There would, Mr Botha believed, be a further constitutional dispensation, reached through direct negotiation – with any parties who foreswore violence – as opposed to the kind of consultative process which led to the creation of the tricameral system.

☐ The system of influx control, one of the corner-stones of separate development, was outdated, too costly and, by implication, no longer acceptable for basic humanitarian reasons.

This had a profound bearing on two of the fundamental mechanisms regulating South African society: the Group Areas Act and its principal control device, the 'pass laws'. The latter were abolished in April 1986; the former remain, at the time of going to press, one of the prime targets of reformists both within and outside Parliament.

☐ Black people who were permanent residents – who did not have homes in the national states – would be granted South African citizenship.

☐ The six national states which have not yet been granted republican status (*see* page 33) would not be pressed to apply for full independence. Implicit in this is that these states may be permitted to rejoin South Africa if they so choose.

The first of these affirmations is probably the most significant. Central to negotiations for a new dispensation is the question of black involvement at national level.

Foreign policy. South Africa belongs in the western camp of nations, maintaining close if not always cordial relations with many (but not all) countries outside the Soviet bloc. Its government generally supports western stances on international issues, but not automatically and certainly not at the expense of South Africa's perceived interests or of her status as a sovereign nation and regional superpower.

Attempts to isolate the Republic from the international community have intensified over the past decade in order to force the pace of political change within the country. Broadly speaking, the protagonists in the offensive are divided into those who believe in what is termed 'constructive engagement' – a policy designed to assist the process of internal reform and resolve external matters (notably the Namibian independence question) through dialogue; and those who urge diplomatic withdrawal and sanctions.

These latter measures would, argue the moderates, cause intolerable hardship within the black community without achieving their political objective, and seriously damage the economies of neighbouring black states.

The Republic is the giant of sub-Saharan Africa. It covers just three per cent of the continent's surface area and is home to a mere five per cent of Africa's total population, yet it accounts for:

☐ 40 per cent of Africa's industrial output;

☐ 25 per cent of gross continental product;

☐ 64 per cent of electricity generated;

☐ 45 per cent of mineral production;

☐ 40 per cent (in normal years) of maize production;

☐ 66 per cent of steel production.

☐ South Africans drive 46 per cent of Africa's motor vehicles and use 36 per cent of its telephones.

The black states within the southern subcontinent rely heavily on and co-operate closely with the Republic. The Rand monetary area encompasses the independent kingdoms of Swaziland and Lesotho as well as the black national states within South Africa. The Customs Union includes the foregoing plus Botswana. A number of regional co-operative bodies have been established (for instance, for collective action on such matters as tourism and environmental conservation).

In 1980 President Botha announced Pretoria's intention to help create a constellation, or confederation, of southern African states, a multilateral order designed to co-ordinate regional growth. Within its terms of reference are the financing of joint industrial and forestry projects; the promotion of private enterprise at the expense of the public sector's rôle; and manpower training. The Development Bank of Southern Africa has an issued share capital of R2 000 million.

South Africa is a member of the United Nations but has not taken part in General Assembly debates since 1974. In 1977 the Security Council imposed a mandatory arms embargo against the Republic and by 1985 several countries, including the United States, had begun to apply limited economic sanctions.

Nevertheless, South Africa remains a member of numerous international agencies (30 inter-governmental and over 700 non-governmental) ranging from finance through medicine to nuclear research.

Defence. Despite the UN embargo, South Africa maintains a well-equipped, powerful defence force – one of the biggest and certainly the most formidable in Africa. Local weapons and equipment manufacture, co-ordinated by the government-owned Armscor organization, has filled most of the gaps created by mandatory military sanctions. The degree of technical sophistication, achieved in a relatively short time, has been impressive by any standards. From South African production lines comes a large range of military vehicles designed to suit local conditions (the Ratel infantry combat carrier and the various mine-proof trucks are noteworthy); new weapons systems (including the R1 rifle, modelled on the Belgian FN; the SS-77 multi-purpose machine-gun; the high-precision G5 155 mm field gun and its mobile version, the G6); tanks (the Olifant); over 200 different types of ammunition; communications systems (the advanced frequency-tapping two-way radio); Impala jet aircraft and a combat helicopter, the Alpha, for the Air Force; mobile strike-craft, armed with guided missiles, for the Navy. Other warships, and submarines, are under development. In fact the country is virtually self-sufficient in terms of its armaments needs. Speculation that South Africa has developed or is developing a nuclear capability has not been given substance.

The Permanent Force within the three services is relatively small (though the Navy and Air Force have a high proportion of professionals). The Army is made up largely of conscripts: white youngsters, on reaching the age of 17, are liable for compulsory national service – the period, at the time of writing, is an onerous two years, with a further 720 days of mandatory territorial service spread over twelve years in the Citizen Force. Thereafter the men are placed in the Active Citizen Force Reserve for a five-year period, and finally into local-defence Commando units.

There are Asian, coloured and black units recruited on a voluntary basis. (The Cape Coloured Corps quota is invariably oversubscribed.)

Most of the South African Defence Force's recent combat experience has been gained in the Namibian border area. These operations at one time included a military presence in southern Angola; in fact, at one stage in the late 1970s, SADF columns fought their way to within a few kilometres of the capital, Luanda, but pulled back under intense diplomatic pressure. Their enemy is the South West Africa Peoples' Organisation (SWAPO). Elsewhere, in search of its other enemies (notably the military wing of the African National Congress) they have mounted pre-emptive and 'hot pursuit' incursions into neighbouring black territories.

Internal security is in the hands of the South African Police. However, elements of the military have in recent times assisted in the control of township unrest, despite vociferous opposition from many quarters.

The legal system. The first settlers at the Cape brought the law of Holland with them: a code evolved from the Germanic laws of western Europe, many of which in turn originated in the *Corpus Juris Civilis*, the four great books prescribed by the Eastern Roman (Byzantine) Emperor Justinian in the sixth century. Despite the systematic Anglicization of the Cape from the early nineteenth century onwards, a Royal Commission found, in 1857, that 'the Roman-Dutch law forms the great bulk of the law in the Colony'. Nevertheless, British influence on the legal system has been considerable, particularly in the realms of court procedure, common law precedent, company and mercantile jurisprudence, and in the rules of evidence.

Overlaying Roman-Dutch common law is the huge and complex body of Statute – parliamentary legislation – that, together, represents possibly the most intricate network of control regulations in the western world. There are, however, moves to de-regulate, to cut down on the amount of restriction and red tape not only in the legal field but also in the administrative, in the interests of freer political and, especially, socio-economic structures.

Ultimate authority is of course vested in Parliament. The subordinate legal structure comprises:

☐ The Appellate Division of the Supreme Court, which sits in Bloemfontein (the country's judicial capital). The Appellate Division, highest of the working courts, is composed of the Chief Justice together with as many appeal judges as the State President may determine.

☐ The Supreme Court, of which there are six provincial divisions (Cape of Good Hope, Eastern Cape, Northern Cape, Orange Free State, Natal and Transvaal), each with a Judge President and State-appointed judges who may be dismissed only by special parliamentary sanction. There are also three local divisions of the Supreme Court (Durban and Coast; Witwatersrand; South-Eastern Cape) presided over by judges.

☐ Other local 'travelling' divisions of the Supreme Court are the Circuit Courts.

☐ The British system of judgement by peers – trial by jury – was established, after the British Occupation, by the first Charter of Justice in 1827. It never proved very successful, however, and was progressively abandoned after the Act of Union in 1910. In 1969, it was formally and completely abolished in favour of a more workable alternative procedure: a single judge or, in serious cases, a judge with two assessors.

☐ Special courts consisting of three judges are appointed from time to time to try cases involving State security.

☐ Lower bodies include magistrates' courts (of which there are 305) which handle the great bulk of routine and minor litigation. Magistrates are public servants appointed by the Minister of Justice, and they perform administrative as well as judicial duties. Many of the more complex and serious cases are heard in the six Regional Magistrates' Courts.

☐ There are also separate Children's Courts, Maintenance Courts, and

☐ Less formal special courts which give judgement in black dis-

THE PROTAGONISTS OF THE '80s.
Key figures in the political cauldron
of South Africa are, on the one hand,
leaders of banned organizations,
foremost among which is the African
National Congress of Nelson Mandela and Oliver Tambo and, on the
other, a diversity of personalities who
have freedom of movement and expression and who range from the
radical left (immediate universal franchise) through the moderate centre
(compromise and controlled reform)
to the radical right (white is might).

The power of the pulpit (1): church-
men Dr. Beyers Naudé, Nobel Peace
Prize-winner Bishop Desmond Tutu
and Dr. Alan Boesak, head of the
World Council of Reformed
Churches and patron of the extra-parliamentary United Democratic Front
– a controversial trio, but representing a significant moral force. Colin
Eglin (2), leader of the moderate and
mostly-white Progressive Federal
Party, the official Parliamentary
Opposition. Chief M.G. Buthelezi

(3), leader of the seven-million-strong Zulu people and of the Inkatha movement, which claims a million members. Helen Suzman (4), Member of Parliament for three decades and a strong voice in the continuing campaign for human rights. President Botha welcomes Alan Hendrickse and Amichand Rajbansi (5), respective leaders of the majority parties in the (Coloured peoples') House of Representatives and the (Indian) House of Delegates. Minister of Law and Order Louis le Grange (6), often at the storm-centre of debate on unrest control. Dr. Nthato Motlana (7) of the Committee of Ten of Soweto, which has been uncompromisingly opposed to local government by appointed blacks. Dr. Jonas Savimbi (8), leader of the Unita guerilla movement in neighbouring Angola and one of the principals in the slow progress towards solving the twin problems of South-West African/Namibian independence and the Cuban presence in Angola. Minister of Constitutional Development Chris Heunis (9 *Centre*), whose portfolio is probably the most important in terms of a possible negotiated political settlement. South Africa's Foreign Minister Pik Botha listens to President Samora Machel of Mozambique speaking of the need for regional peace and co-operation on the sub-continent (10). The two countries signed the Nkomati Accord in 1984.

putes according to indigenous custom. These are presided over by a chief or headman; appeals against decisions may be made to a Commissioner's Court. A Commissioner has the status of a magistrate but is invariably expert in traditional black jurisprudence.

Less than three per cent of persons accused of criminal wrongs had until recently been legally represented in court, largely because of the sheer volume of 'routine' cases – those involving, for instance, identity documents and traffic violations. It is estimated that some 18 million people were arrested for pass law offences between 1916 and 1985. In September of the latter year, however, the President's Council recommended a radical revision of the pass system, and in April of the following year they were formally abolished.

THE ECONOMY

South Africa is an uncomfortable mix of First World sophistication and Third World underdevelopment. On the one hand it has immense natural resources, employs advanced technologies and supports complex industrial and commercial structures. On the other, educational standards among many of the people are low; there are too few jobs and services for the rapidly expanding population and the 'poverty cycle', if not as horrific as it is in some other African countries, does exist, threatening stability and profoundly affecting the process of economic decision-making.

Relative to all this are two recent and highly significant changes of direction, shifts in policy designed to strengthen free market forces and generally to expand the productive base. An explanation of their respective backgrounds is relevant.

In many ways the South African economy is organized along socialistic lines. In the past the emphasis has been on State control; Government has been far and away the largest single employer and the most prolific spender; taxation is high; private initiative has been inhibited and sometimes strangled by red-tape regulation.

Providing intention is translated into decisive action, that will change. A monolithic government presence in the body economic was tolerable enough, perhaps, in good times, when gold rode high, the Rand monetary unit was strong and there was the appearance of financial and social stability. But the economy began to slide, steeply, into recession in 1984; Draconian measures to balance the budget, halt inflation and improve the balance of payments, which had looked set for success for a time, were torpedoed by political unrest in 1985. Meanwhile, the country still needed to create some 300 000 new jobs and build half a million houses a year just to keep pace with minimum black needs – not to mention schools, hospitals, community services and pensions (for the last item, an estimated annual R10 billion, at current rates, will be needed by the end of the century).

Against this background a tentative move has been made to dismantle the apparatus of State ownership, to transfer large sections of present government obligation to the private sector. Specific targets are some of the huge para-statal bodies such as the Iron and Steel Corporation (ISCOR), the Electricity Supply Commission (ESCOM), State transport undertakings (road, rail and air), health services, housing, education and social services (privatization would act to make pensions portable and more individualized).

Parallel to this trend is a relaxation of controls on urban drift (see page 40). Apart from its political sensitivity, influx control has been seen to have had damaging socio-economic consequences. Many of the legal barriers have come down. Also under official attack are the rigid and unrealistically high community standards of the past. The accents now are on self-help housing – 'site-and-service' – schemes; closer involvement of the private sector; and

encouragement of the 'informal economy', a euphemism for back-yard industry and minimally regulated trading. These developments are fundamental: inducement rather than coercion is now the mechanism of mobility in an under-employed and changing society.

Economic pointers. During the first half of the 1980s the most significant contributions to the Gross Domestic Product were made by manufacturing industry (about 22 per cent), mining (13 per cent), commerce (11 per cent), transport and communications (7,5 per cent), electricity and water (four per cent). Agriculture accounts for about five per cent.

These figures reveal the dramatic transformation from an agrarian-based economy a century ago, before the discovery and exploitation of diamonds and gold, to today's advanced industrialization. For much of the twentieth century mining provided the impetus; after the Second World War there was an impressive growth of manufacturing activity. That sector is now the priority: it is capable of much further expansion (South Africa exports too many raw materials that could be fabricated, turned into semi-manufactured or end products) and of absorbing more job-seekers than all the other economic areas put together. This is the vital consideration.

The economy, as mentioned, suffered a number of serious setbacks in the mid-1980s. South Africa is a trading nation (60 per cent of the GDP is represented by the reciprocal flow of goods and services) and is consequently sensitive to international financial pressures. The flexible exchange rate introduced at the beginning of the decade led to rapid short-term growth, but also to a deterioration in the balance of payments on the capital account. Foreign debt accumulated; the Rand failed to rise above its apparent equilibrium level, and sudden loss of international banking confidence following widespread internal unrest and President Botha's unexpectedly conservative reaction to events led, in September 1985, to a brief closure of the Johannesburg Stock Exchange, a moratorium on foreign debt repayments and the re-introduction of the two-tier (financial and commercial Rand) exchange structure.

These developments produced some of the major dilemmas facing the country's policy-makers. On the one hand they created severe constraints on medium and long-term growth (when a government re-schedules its debt, future loans become much more difficult to negotiate with the once-bitten bankers); while on the other, internal pressures demand steady growth. Options are limited, but they include the introduction of import barriers behind which the economy can be artificially stimulated. The major predictable results of a protectionist policy will be a higher inflation rate – justifiable if the job-creation rate also rises – and, since the country will in the years to come have to depend on domestic savings rather than on foreign loans to finance development, a new tax structure, one that will encourage investment and capital formation.

Mining. South Africa has the largest known reserves of gold, platinum, high-grade chromium, manganese, vanadium, fluorspar and andalusite in the world, and massive deposits of diamonds, iron-ore, coal, uranium, asbestos, nickel and phosphates – a powerful litany of natural endowment which places the Republic in the global strategic front line.

Gold production averages some 700 tons a year – roughly 70 per cent of the free world's output. Bullion prices fluctuate, sometimes dramatically; in 1983 South Africa sold over R10 000 million-worth of the yellow metal. Its gold mines are the third largest of the world's suppliers of uranium, a co-product.

Diamonds, discovered in the deep kimberlite pipes of the northern Cape, launched the country's industrial revolution in the 1870s and generated fabulous wealth over the decades that followed. The country is the world's largest producer of gem diamonds – and of the platinum group of metals (palladium, rhodium, iridium, ruthenium as well as platinum itself). About three-quarters of the earth's reserves of both platinum and chromium are locked into the immense Pre-Cambrian strata of South Africa's bushveld complex.

Probably the most important of the strategic minerals is manganese, vital in the production of steel and found in great quantity (about 80 per cent of the world's known reserves, in fact) in the north-western Cape.

Finally there is coal, of which South Africa has located deposits amounting to 56 billion tons, and which provides the country with much of its electricity and synthetic petroleum (see below). The 100 mines produce about 130 million tons (1983 value: R2 000 million) a year, a figure projected to rise to 330 million tons by the year 2000. A healthy proportion of output is exported, most of it through the east coast port of Richards Bay and mainly to northern Europe and Japan, earning South Africa around R1 000 million a year in foreign funds.

Energy. Despite the lack of operating oil-fields, the Republic is a net exporter of energy. Coal, as mentioned above, is the principal source: 60 per cent of coal-mining output is applied to the generation of electricity; 17 per cent to the production of synthetic fuels; six per cent to conversion to coke and tar. Three great oil-from-coal plants have been built: Sasol 1 in the Orange Free State, completed in 1955; Sasols 2 and 3 at Secunda in the eastern Transvaal, the impetus for the latter two coming from the international oil crisis of 1973. Together, these establishments consume 32 million tons of coal a year and represent the world's first and as yet only commercially viable large-scale synthetic fuel operation. Eventually they and others like them will make South Africa self-sufficient in liquid and gas fuels and a host of other coal-based products.

The Electricity Supply Commission (ESCOM), which operates 20 coal-fired, three hydro-electric and two gas-turbine power-stations, provides 93 per cent of electricity consumed (some 120 000 million kilowatts annually). Six new coal-fired stations were coming on stream in the mid-1980s, including one, the largest of its kind in the world, at Matimba in the northern Transvaal.

Supplementary power is provided by the Koeberg nuclear reactors near Cape Town, built by a French consortium and productive from 1985. Their generating capacity is 1 800 megawatts. The plant uses South African uranium enriched by an advanced and highly efficient process developed by South African nuclear scientists.

Strong indications of viable offshore oil and gas fields have been located south of Mossel Bay in the southern Cape.

Industry. A large pool of labour, a wealth of natural resources, technological expertise and, not least, economic and perhaps political necessity are leading South Africa towards self-reliance in industrial products.

In the first half of the 1980s manufacturing industry employed about 1,5 million people and, as has been noted, contributed about a quarter of the Gross Domestic Product.

Government's policy for some years was on decentralization, part of its overall programme of separate development and influx control. Industry, it was felt, had become too concentrated in four major areas: the vast Pretoria-Witwatersrand-Vaal Triangle complex; Durban-Pinetown; the Cape Peninsula; and Port Elizabeth-Uitenhage in the eastern Cape. Industrialists have been encouraged through a series of financial incentives to set up business in the less developed regions, close to or within the black national states, in order to spread wealth more evenly and help stem the flow of job-seekers to the cities. By and large the policy has not been as successful as Government could have wished, and the whole question of urban concentration is under active review (see previous page).

The larger manufacturing sectors include:

☐ *Metal industries.* The Iron and Steel Corporation has three major plants which together produce about six million tons of liquid steel a year, with specialized metal products (for instance carbon and stainless steel, ferro-alloys, copper and brass, high-carbon chrome) turned out by a number of smaller mills. The country's engineering and heavy industrial works manufacture everything from cranes and sugar mills through engines, turbines, machine tools, agricultural equipment, structural steel and cables to specialized industrial machinery and computer products.

☐ *Non-metallic mineral products* (largely for the construction industry) were running at an annual value of about R4 000 million in the early 1980s.

☐ *Transport and equipment.* There are a number of vehicle manufacturing and assembly plants in the country, most in and around Port Elizabeth, the 'Detroit of South Africa'. In the early 1980s their combined output was some 400 000 units a year (local content is 66 per cent), though the industry has suffered grievously during the mid-decade recession. Heavy duty diesel engines for buses are manufactured in Cape Town; gearboxes in Boksburg in the Transvaal.

☐ *Chemicals and pharmaceuticals.* The list of basic industrial chemicals produced in South Africa is long, ranging across the entire spectrum from fertilizers and pesticides through explosives to petroleum products, plastics and paints.

☐ *Food products.* Again, practically the whole range is locally processed. The industry's output was worth R10 000 million in 1983 and it employed 180 000 people. Some 60 per cent of production is exported, principally to EEC countries.

☐ *Clothing and textiles.* With an annual production value of R4 000 million in the first half of the decade, this industry employs eight per cent of the total workforce and, because of its labour intensity, is earmarked as one of the key growth points.

Transport and communications. South Africa's infrastructure is the continent's most developed – an important factor in the general scheme of foreign relations and international pressures. Many of the countries of the subcontinent depend heavily, even for survival, on the Republic's road and rail network.

☐ There are some 190 000 kilometres of roads interlacing the country, 50 000 kilometres of which have been surfaced, together with a further 50 000 kilometres of roadworks within the urban areas. Pride of the system are the National routes, comparable to West Germany's famed autobahns. They are used by almost five million vehicles – but not, relatively speaking, very safely: the road death toll is one of the highest in the world.

☐ Railways – 36 000 kilometres of track, of which 20 000 kilometres are electrified – are run by an umbrella body, the South African Transport Services, the largest commercial enterprise in the country. SATS also operates the national airline (SAA), the road transport services, the harbours and the pipelines. Parts of the conglomerate may be privatized in terms of the government's recently stated policy to allow free market forces greater play.

Efficient suburban networks service Pretoria-Witwatersrand, Durban-Pinetown and, especially, the Cape Peninsula. Rolling-stock is locally manufactured.

45

Luxury travel is represented by the renowned Blue Train (two trains, in fact) which plies elegantly between Pretoria and Cape Town. SATS plans to introduce high-speed (200 kilometre per hour) inter-city trains.

The railways handle some 800 million passengers and 200 million tons of freight each year.

☐ South African Airways operates a fleet of wide-bodied Boeings on international flights to Europe, the Americas (Houston, New York, Rio, Buenos Aires), the Far East (Hong Kong, Taipei) and to Tel Aviv. There are also some 500 internal flights a week.

Twenty private airlines fly 80 routes to 50 South African centres. Licensed aerodromes number 230; Durban, Cape Town and Pretoria-Johannesburg (Jan Smuts lies between the two cities) have international airports.

Agriculture. The Republic is one of only half a dozen or so of the world's net food-exporting countries – a testament in a sense to the expertise of its farming community and water engineers because the subcontinent's natural land resources are poor. Rainfall is mostly seasonal and invariably – certainly in recent years – unpredictable. The soil is not especially fertile: erosion over the millennia and the leaching of Africa's earth during the wetter periods of the continent's history have impoverished the nutrient content over large areas (only 12 per cent of the surface area is arable).

Despite these built-in drawbacks the country has doubled its agricultural output since 1960, and now exports, in an averagely good year, over R2 000 million-worth of meat and produce.

The diversity of the country's climatic conditions (*see* page 7) enables its farmers to grow a wide variety of crops, from the sugar and subtropical fruits of Natal through the huge maize yields of the summer rainfall areas to the tobacco of the more arid regions; and to rear livestock for beef, pork and dairy products, mutton and wool.

Gross annual value of all agricultural output during the first part of the 1980s hovered around the R8 000 million mark. A succession of droughts and escalating input costs, however, placed large sections of the white farming fraternity under severe financial strain. The situation in the less developed and generally less well-endowed black rural areas tended to deteriorate more rapidly under the adverse conditions and in places reached critical proportions.

Labour. The entire structure of labour and labour relations in South Africa underwent a radical transformation following the acceptance of recommendations contained in the seminal reports of the Wiehahn and Riekert commissions of inquiry in the late 1970s (*see* page 35). These made provision for full freedom of association of all classes of urban worker (that is to say, they included migrants and commuters from the national states); the registration of trade unions; participation in a formal collective bargaining process; the right to strike; the abolition of job reservation (and, in the giant mining industry, the elimination of all discrimination in the workplace on the basis of race); the establishment of industrial councils and of extensive training programmes, a comprehensive code regulating conditions of work, minimum wages and social benefits. The Riekert Commission's recommendations also pre-empted the abolition of influx control and the encouragement of private enterprise in the 'informal economy' (*see* page 44).

Against the background of over-restrictive labour control that has been a feature of the economy since the early mining days, all this was progress indeed. Black workers have been quick to organize and to prove themselves highly skilled in the cut-and-thrust arena of industrial negotiation.

The unions are a powerful force in the political as well as economic field but, at the time of writing, largely a latent one in the former: their principal concern remains the welfare and material advancement of the workforce. Late in 1985, however, the various unions and groups of unions (with two major exceptions) came together under COSATU, an umbrella federation. Initially COSATU represented around half a million workers, and indications are that it will use its considerable bargaining muscle to help redress political grievances.

THE ARTS, SPORT AND RECREATION

Culturally, and in the realms of leisure, entertainment and sport, South Africa offers as varied and pleasing a fare as any other middle-sized western country, and perhaps more so. Its special prides are the game and nature reserves, and the mostly beautiful and often spectacular landscapes. For the visitor, there is a great deal to see and do; the tourist industry is well organized; holiday-makers are able to stay in and travel round the Republic in comfort and, at rates of exchange prevailing at the time of writing, to do so relatively cheaply.

The arts. The scene is lively, and much of it of international standard. Literature, the visual arts, theatre, ballet, opera and symphonic music thrive enthusiastically in South Africa's major centres.

Much of the activity falls within the ambit of the four State-sponsored performing arts councils. Together they employ over 2 000 artists and theatre technicians and stage around 300 shows of one sort or another each year in a variety of splendid buildings. Most notable of these are probably the grand Nico Malan theatre-complex in Cape Town (opera house, drama theatre, three smaller auditoriums and a full resident orchestra), Pretoria's State Theatre and Bloemfontein's new Opera House.

Excellent independent (independent of the arts councils, that is) symphony orchestras are based and give regular performances in Durban, Johannesburg and Cape Town. Also among the more outstanding of the non-governmental enterprises are the Baxter Theatre complex near Cape Town's university and the Market Theatre in Johannesburg.

Music of a different kind – a unique kind – is emerging from the black urban community, a vibrant synthesis of African and western idioms that is beginning to make its mark beyond the borders of the townships.

South Africa has produced more than its share of gifted instrumentalists, opera singers and ballet dancers. The country, though, finds it difficult to retain its own: universities and other learning centres turn out an unusual wealth of young talent which is often lost to the more sophisticated stages and concert halls of Europe and America.

Radio and television services are comparatively extensive – compared, that is to say, with the size of the population. There are four national television stations with a fifth – a subscriber (cable) service run by private enterprise – planned. Radio was rationalized in 1985 and the number of national stations slightly reduced: there is one English service, one Afrikaans, one popular-music (Radio Five), one classical-music (Radio Allegro), and a plethora of African-language, regional and national-state stations.

South Africa can claim few literary giants of the kind that one might expect to have emerged in a country of such beauty, complexity, conflict and tragedy. There has been no Steinbeck to give voice to the wrath of the economically underprivileged; no James Baldwin to bring fiery articulation to ethnic consciousness; no Orwell, no Solzhenitsyn. It could, though, be that very complexity that inhibits the pen. Says Nadine Gordimer, a leading contemporary novelist: 'Living in a society that has been as deeply and calculatedly compartmentalised as South Africa's has been under the colour bar, the writer's potential has unscalable limitations.'

Nevertheless, there have been and are South African writers of real stature: the much under-estimated Olive Schreiner; the eccentric Roy Campbell; the mystic Eugene Marais, and, of recent vintage, Alan Paton and Lourens van der Post who each, in his own way, has bared the soul of his beloved country; Nadine Gordimer and Jan Coetzee; André Brink and Etienne Leroux; the brilliant Athol Fugard and his fellow playwright Gibson Kente. Among the black people there is, too, a powerful tradition of oral literature: the key to their past, and perhaps the door to the country's literary future.

Sport. South Africans are a sport-loving people, the white community almost to the point of fanaticism. Rugby comes close to being an obsession among Afrikaans-speakers, and the Springbok sides over most of the past seven decades have generally been regarded as unofficial world champions. Cricket comes a close second. Football reigns supreme within the black community: there are 10 000 soccer clubs and 600 000 soccer players in South Africa. Track athletics and, especially, marathon and ultra-long distance running are rapidly gaining in across-the-board popularity. World-class record-breaking athletes have emerged (Sidney Maree; Zola Budd), as well as great cricketers (Pollock, Barlow, Richards, Procter); rugby players (too many of them to enumerate); footballers; boxers; motor-cyclists; golfers (Gary Player); and tennis stars (Kevin Curren). But South Africa has been isolated with increasing severity from the mainstream of international sport, despite the country's strenuous attempts to 'put its house in order' and integrate sport at all levels (government regulation has been eliminated; practically every sports body and sportsman supports the non-racial approach).

The Gleneagles Agreement binds governments to discourage their sporting nationals from visiting South Africa. Most of the western democracies have stopped short of imposing formal bans, relying on moral pressure instead. In 1985 a watershed decision was handed down by a New Zealand court: it forbade the planned All Blacks rugby tour on the club-constitutional grounds that the tour would not be in the best interests of New Zealand rugby. The following year a Kiwi invitation side, the Cavaliers, toured South Africa, but it did not officially represent New Zealand and, although accusations of professionalism were hotly denied, there is no doubt that financial incentives will in future play an increasingly part in luring top-class teams to this country.

The fundamental of the matter is that amateur sport can no longer be dissociated from politics, and only when governmental structures become acceptable to the international community will South African sportsmen be allowed back into the fold. Meanwhile, more and more of the country's shining young stars play tennis and cricket and burn the athletics tracks in adopted colours.

Game parks and nature reserves. There are at present 14 national parks and almost 500 smaller (some very small) reserves run by regional and local authorities in southern Africa.

Biggest and most famed is the Kruger National Park in the Lowveld of the north-eastern corner of the country – a long, narrowish 20 000 square-kilometre stretch of bushveld the size of Wales, bounded in the south by the Crocodile River, in the east by Mozambique, in the north by the Limpopo and in the west by the lovely eastern Transvaal lowlands. Close to its western border are a dozen and more private reserves, many in the luxury class.

This is big game country. The Kruger has 137 species of mammal, including the 'big five' – elephant (10 000 of them), lion, leopard, buffalo (30 000), rhino, immense numbers of antelope (including 100 000 impala), 450 species of bird, 114 of reptile, 40 of fish, 33 of amphibian and 227 species of butterfly. There are 15 rest-camps – the larger ones virtual villages of comfortable, thatched rondavels (all mod cons) clustered around a central complex of restaurant and shops – and 1 880 kilometres of tarred or well-gravelled roads that lead visitors to water-holes, picnic spots and grand viewing-sites.

For all the magnificence of raw Africa that it encloses, the Kruger National Park is designed for the comfort-conscious family group – the idea being to allow as many South Africans as possible to enjoy their natural heritage. It succeeds admirably in its objective. At peak period the park accommodates, entertains and informs 3 000 visitors on a daily basis.

Other parks and reserves worthy of special mention are:
□ The scenically lovely Golden Gate Highlands National Park. Situated in the Orange Free State some 360 kilometres south of Johannesburg, the park has an attractive variety of wildlife (mainly buck) and is notable for its birds of prey.
□ The Mountain Zebra National Park, located in the Great Karoo region on the northern slopes of the Bankberg range west of Cradock, is haven to this rare, at one time almost extinct, species. Twenty years ago there were just 25 of the animals in existence; today between 200 and 300 roam the sweet-thorn and succulent-covered slopes of the park.
□ The Addo Elephant National Park was established in the 1930s to protect the last of the great herds of the eastern Cape. Situated about 70 kilometres north of Port Elizabeth, its tangled vegetation and low tree-cover sustain a three-fold higher density of elephant population than any other tract of land in Africa, together with black rhino, a variety of antelope and some 170 species of bird.
□ Similarly, the Bontebok National Park in the south-western Cape, close to Swellendam, was launched to rescue the species (its cousin, the bluebuck, became extinct in the early nineteenth century). The original breeding herd numbered just 17 animals; today the bontebok population is well established. Bird life here, too, is prolific: over 180 species have been identified.
□ The two Tsitsikamma national parks – the Forest and the Coastal – sprawl along the southern Cape's attractive Garden Route. The former was proclaimed in order to preserve the dense, deep-green, ancient yellowwoods (one specimen is 37 metres tall and has a 30-metre spread), candlewoods and assegais. There are something over 30 tree species, a thick undergrowth of ferns and lichens and some of the country's finest walking and hiking trails in and around the park.

The Coastal Reserve is designed to protect both the marine life and the shoreline of lovely cliffs, river gorges and rich vegetation of yellowwood, fern, orchid, protea and myriad species of lily.
□ The Karoo National Park is situated near Beaufort West, 48 kilometres north-east of Cape Town. The Great Karoo, an arid but hauntingly beautiful region, has a unique dwarf vegetation which the park helps preserve.
□ The Kalahari Gemsbok National Park, almost 100 000 hectares in extent, is South Africa's second biggest reserve. A wilderness of red dunes and dry riverbeds, sparse grass and thornbush, it lies between Namibia and Botswana. Despite the general lack of water, huge herds of antelope – blue wildebeest, springbok, eland, gemsbok – thrive. They have adapted their feeding habits, supplementing their diet with moisture-bearing desert plants such as tsamma melon and wild cucumber.
□ The Augrabies Falls National Park lies astride the Orange River west of the lonely town of Upington, and is renowned for its mag-

nificent waterfalls and gorge. The former plunge more than 90 metres, first in a series of steps and then in one final great leap.

☐ The Royal Natal National Park – which, despite its name, is controlled by the Natal Parks Board and not by the national body – lies within the high fastness of the Drakensberg range, its western extremity bordering on Lesotho. Famed more for its scenic splendour and mountaineering (walking as well as climbing) attractions than for its wildlife, it nevertheless offers much to the naturalist: immense forests of yellowwood; wild orchid, gladioli, aloes, ancient cycads and the brilliance of everlastings. There is a fascinating variety of birdlife, including three of the world's seven species of crane and an impressive number of raptors – jackal buzzard, martial eagle, black eagle and the rare and beautiful lammergeyer that makes its home in the highest of the cloud-combed peaks.

☐ Indeed, the Natal and Zululand game reserves, run by dedicated teams of scientists and conservationists, are some of the most impressive in Africa. The climate is invariably warm to hot, humid in the lower areas; the terrain is lush, with an astonishing variety of woodland, forest, savannah, thornveld, riverine and grassland plant species. Hluhluwe Game Reserve, for instance, is just six per cent of the size of the Kruger National Park but harbours 68 per cent of the total number of the Kruger's species. Game – from lion through rhino to a score of antelope species – is prolific. Apart from Hluhluwe, reserves well worth a visit include Mkuzi, Ndumu (wonderful numbers of tropical birds), Umfolozi (home to the once-threatened white rhino) and St Lucia (hippopotamus and crocodile). Most spectacular of Natal's parks is probably Giant's Castle Game Reserve, which encompasses the 3 207-metre high massif of the Castle itself as well as the lovely forests and sandstone cliffs of the Injasuti Valley.

South Africa's parks and reserves are permanent features of a subcontinent that, in so many other respects, is undergoing the trauma of rapid change. This is an age of transition; society and its institutions are being restructured; the process could be long and painful; the outcome is uncertain. But there is comfort in the knowledge that, whatever else the future holds, the country will still and always have its precious natural heritage, its stunning diversity of scenic splendour, its far horizons.

Study in contrasts. Johannesburg, one of the world's mining and financial capitals, is aggressively modern, vibrant, brash. But for all the surface sophistication there is still something of its rugged digger origins about the place, seen in the random architecture and sensed in the life-styles of its citizens.

1

2

Johannesburg is barely a century old: a hundred years ago the area was a silent, sunlit stretch of near-virgin highveld that sustained a scatter of kraals, the occasional lonely farmstead and very little else. But in 1886 an Australian drifter named George Harrison accidentally stumbled on the world's richest treasure-house of gold beneath the 'ridge of white waters' – the Witwatersrand. Today the city (1) is at the epicentre of one of Africa's greatest conurbations, a bustling, polyglot metropolis surrounded by dense rings of satellite towns which, together, generate some 60 per cent of the country's wealth. Central Johannesburg has lost much of its commercial glitter to the vigorous new suburbs in recent years but there are imaginative plans to restyle the business district.

3

6

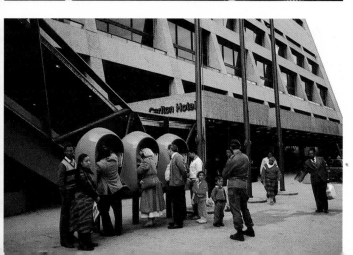

Despite Johannesburg's wealth, and there is a great deal of it, for the majority of Witwatersrand residents life remains a struggle – to make ends meet, to obtain and hold on to a job and a decent place to live; and, as patient commuter queues illustrate (2), to get to and from work on an overloaded public transport system. Nearby is Diagonal Street, home of the Johannesburg Stock Exchange (3), which contrasts sharply with one of the comparatively few remaining city-centre buildings that date back to Johannesburg's infant years (4), a ramshackle home to an Indian family, part of a small but remarkably unified minority. One of the city's focal points is the Carlton Centre (5 & 6), a giant hotel, office and shopping complex. The Centre's observation deck offers commanding views of the city and its surrounds.

Suburban panorama. Modern, upmarket shopping centres are a feature of Johannesburg's suburbia, especially in the wealthier, mainly northern parts. Rosebank, with its imaginative shopping malls and alfresco eateries (1), is but one example of the movement of business away from the city centre. Focus of the very affluent Sandton area and arguably the most impressive development of all, however, is Sandton City (2 & 3) with its magnificent hotel, complete with glass-and-gold atrium (4).

Not all of Johannesburg, though, is brand new: one of the mansions of the early mining magnates (5) is a reminder of a more sedate era, while the entrance to the Great Hall of the University of the Witwatersrand (6) is symbolic of a proud academic heritage. Busiest of Johannesburg's suburbs is Hillbrow (7), a high-rise concentration of apartment blocks, nose-to-tail traffic and all-night life. Home to some 90 000 people drawn from a variety of ethnic groups, Hillbrow is the densest residential area in the southern hemisphere. However, only a stone's throw away are broad tree-lined avenues, spacious homes, sculptured gardens, and swimming pools (8).

1

2

3

4

7

8

Leisure time. Johannesburgers love their sport, as do most South Africans. Among the whites, the national game, perhaps the national obsession, is rugby, and despite virtual exclusion from the international arena the country still manages to produce some of the world's finest players. The new Ellis Park stadium (1 & 3) can accommodate about 90 000 spectators. The ground is also used for soccer, which has an enormous following, especially within the black community – there are 10 000 football clubs and some 600 000 players in South Africa. But horse-racing was the first of Johannesburg's sporting preoccupations, drawing the crowds while diggers' tents still littered the veld. Today gold and the turf still co-exist, but instead of tents a huge mine headgear provides the backdrop to an afternoon at the races (4 & 5). Among the many gentler pursuits are visits to the Zoo (2) and its lake, and to the Santarama miniature city (6), modelled on the famed Madurodam in Holland. Santarama has a scale 1:25, and its patrons are charmed by the splendid musical fountain.

1

2

3

4

Every South African urban complex has its high-density black townships. In the early days they were called 'locations', and until quite recently their people were, for the most part, classed as 'temporary' residents and deemed to belong in traditional 'homelands'. That is all changing, though the transition brings its own discomforts. Blacks may now own houses under long-lease or freehold title; the whole thorny issue of influx control – an unsuccessful and painful attempt to halt urban drift – is subject to radical revision; there is a move towards general de-regulation and the encouragement of an informal economy (cottage and backyard industry). Soweto (1-7) is by far the largest of South Africa's black townships, officially accommodating a little over a million people, unofficially perhaps twice that number. Sprawling, grimy, dreary for the most part, it does have its better houses, paved roads, street lighting; its shops, pubs, shebeens and an animation all its own.

South Africa has produced nearly half the world's gold over the past decades, and is currently responsible for 60 per cent of the free world's output. Other metals and minerals contribute substantially to the national wealth: 59 in all are mined or quarried, including large and strategically valuable quantities of manganese, platinum and chromium (of which South Africa has the largest of the earth's known deposits); diamonds, coal, uranium, asbestos, nickel and phosphates.

1

2

3

Gold mining is for the most part labour-intensive, with the majority of workers coming as migrants from national states within the borders of South Africa: for example, the Transkei, Ciskei, KwaZulu and Bophuthatswana. They also come from Mozambique, Botswana, Lesotho, Swaziland and Malawi – and are important foreign exchange earners for these countries. Among the biggest and deepest mines in the world are those near Carletonville on the Far West Rand – at Western Deep Levels, for example, gold is being won 3 780 metres below the surface.

4

Nearby, the huge operations at East and West Driefontein provide a glimpse of a day on the mines: learning to lay tracks at the mine's training school (1), drilling deep underground (3), pouring the molten metal (4), cleaning ingots (5) and coming off shift (6 & 8) at the end of a tough but comparatively well-paid day to a meal in the canteen (2). On most mines, sporting and recreational facilities are excellent, while pursuits such as traditional dancing (7) are also popular.

Seat of government. South Africa has three capitals: Cape Town (legislative); Bloemfontein (judicial); and Pretoria, the country's administrative headquarters, a city that nestles comfortably among the eastern foothills of the Magaliesberg. Some 60 kilometres north of frenetic Johannesburg, Pretoria is a quiet, well laid out, dignified town of jacaranda-lined streets, neat gardens, public parks (over 100 of them), monuments and some fine buildings, two of the more notable being the neo-classical Palace of Justice (1), and the Union Buildings (5 & 6), which preside over the city from Meintjeskop, highest of the surrounding hills. Designed by the renowned architect Herbert Baker, the Union Buildings were completed in 1913 and served as a model for the grander but no more attractive Raj legislature in New Delhi. Atop another of Pretoria's hills is the imposing University of South Africa (4), a non-residential institution with a huge enrolment. Tuition is entirely by correspondence. Despite its slower pace, however, the city is not without its bustle of traffic, pedestrians and shopping centres (2, 3, 7 & 8).

7

8

Jacaranda city. Pretoria is famed for its 50 000-plus, vividly colourful jacaranda trees (1), the first two of which were imported from Rio de Janeiro in 1888. Just outside the city on yet another hilltop is the Voortrekker Monument (2 & 3), started in 1938 and completed in 1949 to commemorate the pioneers of the Great Trek. It comprises a cenotaph, lower hall and Hall of Heroes, whose interior walls display an impressive 92-metre-long frieze depicting the main events of the Trek.

The Treaty of Vereeniging, which brought to an end the long, bloody and mutually exhausting war between Boer and Briton, was signed on 31 May, 1902 in Pretoria's gracious Melrose House (6), Lord Kitchener's residence at the time, later High Commissioner Lord Milner's and now a beautifully preserved showpiece. Focal point of the Transvaal's performing arts is the State Theatre (4) — modern, luxuriously appointed and equipped.

Pretoria's Fountains Valley Park (5), complete with miniature railway (7), is a popular venue for a family braai — the barbecue is a national institution, but the convenience of a gas cooker is making inroads on the traditional wood-coal fire.

Northern playground. Legal restrictions on gambling – and censorship generally – in many of the national states within and adjoining the Republic are minimal. Glittering hotels and casinos play host to tens of thousands of South Africans as well as visitors from abroad. Most popular is Sun City (1-5), an enormous and gleefully materialistic concrete-and-tinsel hotel complex that offers roulette, blackjack and the ubiquitous one-armed bandit; imported big-name entertainers, wining, dining, lavish cabaret and *risqué* films; world title fights, golf, watersports and poolside relaxation on an island of green grass, palm trees and crystal clear fountains surrounded by dry, dusty thornveld. Sun City is in

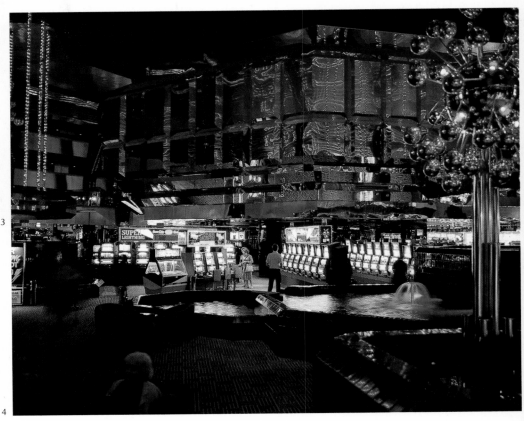

the national state of Bophuthatswana and a comfortable three-hour drive from Pretoria and Johannesburg. Most of the hotel-casino developments are oases of luxury, and valuable revenue-earners, in otherwise poverty-stricken lands. Bophuthatswana - comprising seven blocks of territory scattered over three of South Africa's four provinces – is one of the luckier states: its deposits of the platinum group of metals are the world's third largest.

1

3

4

The northern parts of the Transvaal are farmlands and flattish bushveld, dominated by massive baobab and mopane trees and stretching to distant hills, most spectacular of which are the Soutpansberg, a 130-kilometre range that divides the northern Lowveld from the high country to the southeast, and whose summit is a fertile, cool plateau settled by the southward-migrating Venda people in the early 18th century. The region is also home to other tribal and national groups, including the North-Sotho and Ndebele. Venda is in fact a national state, albeit a miniscule one of just 6 000 square kilometres and a population of fewer than half a million, 50 000 of whom earn their living (and provide much of Venda's national income) as migrant workers in South Africa.

A rural miscellany. Venda women at their riverside chores (1). A North-Sotho farm labourer, her child safe and asleep on her back (2). Part of the Honnet Nature Reserve (3), between the Soutpansberg and the Limpopo River. Sunflowers (4), one of the area's most profitable commercial crops and a valuable source of vegetable oil. Sotho baskets for sale at a roadside (6). An Ndebele kraal (5) and Ndebele girls (7) in traditional dress.

5

6

7

2

1

3

5

4

The edge of the Escarpment. A waterfall plunges down from the 2 127-metre high Wolkberg (1) at the head of the Magoebaskloof, one of the loveliest, most fertile parts of the country. An especially fine scenic drive is the 97-kilometre road that leads through these spectacular hills and valleys from Pietersburg to Tzaneen, dropping 600 metres in one six-kilometre stretch of thick, dark-green woodland. Sawmills are a feature of the area and although timber plantations abound – such as the one around the Magoebaskloof Dam (2) – the upper slopes are graced by glades of indigenous trees: red stinkwood, ironwood, yellowwood, cabbage tree and the superb 'rooihout' *(Ochna o'connorii)*. Above the dam is the Debegeni waterfall (5), the name meaning 'place of the big pot', a reference to the pool at the foot of the cascade. Fruit and winter vegetables are part of the agricultural bounty of Magoebaskloof and tea is also grown extensively (3 & 4) – the plantations began in 1963 with the help of Kenyan expertise and Industrial Development Corporation money.

1

The splendours of the Transvaal Drakensberg. The Great Escarpment runs north to south for 300 kilometres through the eastern Transvaal, a jagged, majestically spectacular range of mountains and chasms dividing Highveld from Lowveld. The Blyde River Canyon (1) is one of the natural wonders of Africa, falling almost sheer for 800 metres from the great flat-topped buttress of Mariepskop and its trio of companion peaks, the Three Rondavels, to the river below. The Blyde River (4), a tributary of the Olifants, takes its name from the Afrikaans word for 'joy'.

It was here, in 1841, that a party of Voortrekker women, believing themselves to be widows when their reconnoitering menfolk failed to return (the women had already named its sister river 'Treur', which means 'sorrow'), were unexpectedly and joyously reunited. One of the main routes of access to the area is via the Abel Erasmus Pass, where russet-leaved mountain syringas (3) clothe the slopes down to the road. Not surprisingly, the region is a mecca for hikers and holiday-makers, the Blydepoort Dam (2) and resort (5) being especially popular.

Spectacular views abound as one follows the eastern Transvaal Escarpment, among them Pinnacle Rock **(1)** and two of the loveliest of many waterfalls, Lisbon **(5)** and Berlin **(6)**. The charming town of Pilgrim's Rest **(2 & 3)** was a thriving little mining community in the 1870s. As one of the Transvaal's first gold-rush towns, it drew diggers from as far afield as California and Australia, and at one time boasted 21 stores, 18 canteens, three bakeries and a spirited, sometimes outrageous, social life. There were some notable finds here (including a 6 038-gram nugget) and at the quaintly named neighbouring sites of Waterfall Gully, Peach Tree

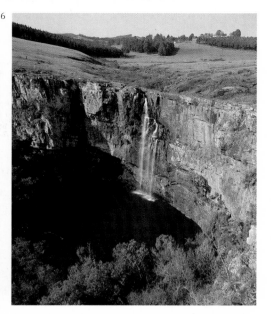

Creek and, farther away, Spitskop and Mac Mac. But gold production began to decline after 1876 and gradually, through the decades, the area was given over to forestry, though a few tiny mines still operate (4) and ever-hopeful prospectors continue to pan the streams. The town itself, now reduced to around 630 souls, remains as it once was, virtually untouched by time, a living museum. Also linked to the region's gold rush lore are the Bourke's Luck Potholes (7), strikingly unusual examples of water erosion at the confluence of the Blyde and Treur rivers. It was here that Tom Bourke panned the river and found a fortune in nuggets.

Looking across the mountains from Long Tom Pass towards Sabie (1). The pass, now tarred, its gradients well planned and a popular tourist drive, was once the ruggedly precarious transport route from the eastern Transvaal centre of Lydenburg to the Portuguese East African port of Lourenço Marques (now Maputo, capital of Mozambique). The pass was named after the huge 'Long Tom' 15 cm-calibre Creusot field guns used with devastating effect against the British during the Anglo-Boer War. In September 1900 General Sir Redvers Buller, advancing northwards after relieving Ladysmith, occupied Lydenburg but met with fierce resistance from the remnants of the Boer forces, whose rearguard action in the tortuous Devil's Knuckles area of the high Transvaal Drakensberg kept the Gordon Highlanders at bay for two costly days.

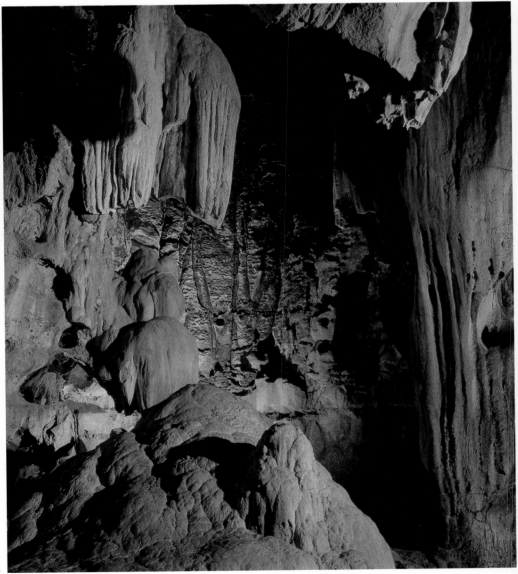

The Sudwala Caves (2 & 3), embedded in a mountain massif known as Mankelekele (which means 'crag on crag'), close to the Crocodile River, are a geological wonder and prime tourist attraction. Rainwater filtering through the dolomite rock over aeons created the lofty chambers of the caves and their festoons of stalagmites and stalactites. One chamber is 90 metres long, 45 metres wide and its formations are of blue, emerald green and pure white. It is said that the labyrinths extend some 30 kilometres.

The stately Elands River Falls **(4)** near Waterval Boven. Here Paul Kruger's Eastern Railway negotiated the Escarpment, linking the Transvaal Republic with the port of Lourenço Marques, now Maputo. Started in 1887 as an attempt to break the British communications stranglehold, it reached the area in 1894 at the cost of countless lives: fever, predatory animals, alcohol and work-gang violence took tragic toll of the workforce. The protected tree fern **(5)** is a common sight in the region.

The eastern Transvaal Lowveld is game country, last sanctuary of the once-teeming hills and plains of the great interior. Biggest of all the country's reserves — larger in extent than Israel — is the world-renowned Kruger National Park, a 19 585 square-kilometre stretch of bushveld sprawling over the north-east part of South Africa that plays host to more than 500 000 visitors a year. Its 15 rest camps, ranging from tiny Roodewal to Skukuza, which is more a self-contained village than a wilderness camp, are designed for comfortable, inexpensive family holidays rather than for the rugged safari. The region is one of the subcontinent's few remaining havens for the big cats.

2

3

4

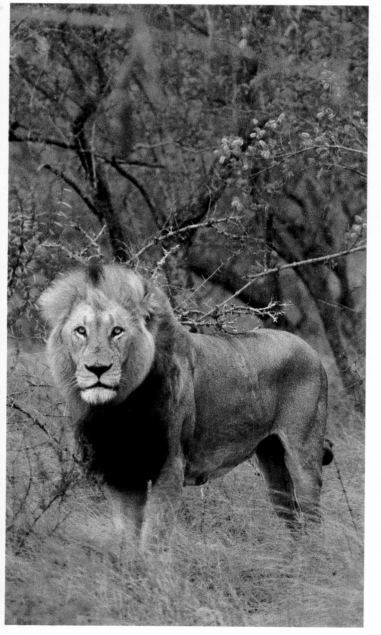

Around 300 cheetahs **(1 & 2)** live in the Kruger National Park. These cousins to the secretive leopard **(3)** are longer-legged, swifter (they can move at up to 110 km/h) and prefer the relatively few patches of open country to dense bush, as they hunt by outrunning prey and need room in which to move. King of the cats, though, is the lion **(4-7)**. This magnificent male **(6)** was photographed in Timbavati, one of a scatter of smaller, privately owned reserves along Kruger's western border. Most of these adjacent reserves are dense with game; their lodges are in the luxury class and cater to the wealthier game viewer. Timbavati is no exception, but has an added attraction – it is one of the few areas that harbours the rare and beautiful white lion **(4)** – not an albino (its eyes have colour, though its coat is snowy) but rather the product of a recessive gene.

The northern segment of the Kruger National Park is the meeting place of a number of Africa's major ecosystems, and the countryside is one of dramatic contrasts: splendid hills, deep valleys and river gorges; wetland and dry bush; thick forest and open plain; lava flat and soft sand. Water is plentiful; the wildlife prolific. Here in the northern park is the lushly-fringed Luvuvhu River (**1**) where the visitor is certain to see nyala, hippo (**4**) and, if lucky, the beautiful but shy bushbuck (**5**). There are about a thousand bushbuck in the Kruger National Park but they are seldom seen as they tend to browse at night, early in the morning and during the late afternoon, and rest up during the day. There is a great deal of variation in size and coloration within the species: about 40 distinct forms are thought to exist, ranging in colour from dark, unmarked brown to spotted and striped chestnut. Birdlife also abounds and the whitefronted bee-eater (**2**), with its dragon-fly prey, is but one of 450 species occurring in the park.

A male waterbuck is a lone intruder as a herd of impala mills around at Orpen Dam (**3**) towards the south of the park. Impala (**see also 6**) are almost synonymous with the Kruger National Park: the park holds around 160 000 of these graceful antelope and visitors tend to take them for granted. They do, though, merit a closer look from game-viewers, both for their agility and their behaviour patterns. An impala can leap three metres high without apparent effort; a startled herd of several hundred will cover the ground as one in a swift, flowing, instinctively choreographed movement that surprises and delights the eye. The group organization is complex: normally gentle and gregarious animals, adult males become fiercely competitive and territorial in the mating season.

The warthog (1) is not the handsomest of Nature's children, but what it lacks in looks it makes up for in toughness and instinct for self-preservation: the tusks are razor-sharp, the senses of smell and hearing acute. Grazers for the most part, these animals can also live on wild fruits, tubers and roots.

A tree leguaan (2) is not pretty either. Leguaans, of which there are two species in southern Africa (the other is the Nile monitor) are prized by local herbalists for the curative properties of their skin and fat. The tree species has a curious defence mechanism: when molested it will feign death rather than attempt escape.

A kudu bull (3) browses in the Kruger National Park. The kudu is among the largest of Africa's antelopes, lives in family groups of about a dozen and, in the mating season, is fiercely territorial: fights between competing bulls can be fatal. The long, spiral horns take about six years to reach their full size.

White rhino (4) occur in the Kruger National Park as well as in the adjacent Londolozi game reserve (part of the extensive Sabie-Sand reserve) where these specimens were photographed. The white rhino is, after the elephant, the second largest of the land mammals, the males weighing up to 3,5 tons. Aggressive enough in looks, the white rhino is not nearly as belligerent as its rarer cousin, the black rhino, though it will mock charge if alarmed.

Wild Dogs (5) are a common sight in the Kruger National Park. These gregarious animals hunt in packs, relentlessly pursuing their quarry until they run it down.

One of the park's major rivers is the Olifants (6). The Olifants rest camp, set on rocky cliffs a full hundred metres above the river, is particularly attractive. Visitors enjoy stunning views of the hills and valleys and (with binoculars) the prolific wildlife drawn to the lush riverine vegetation.

5

6

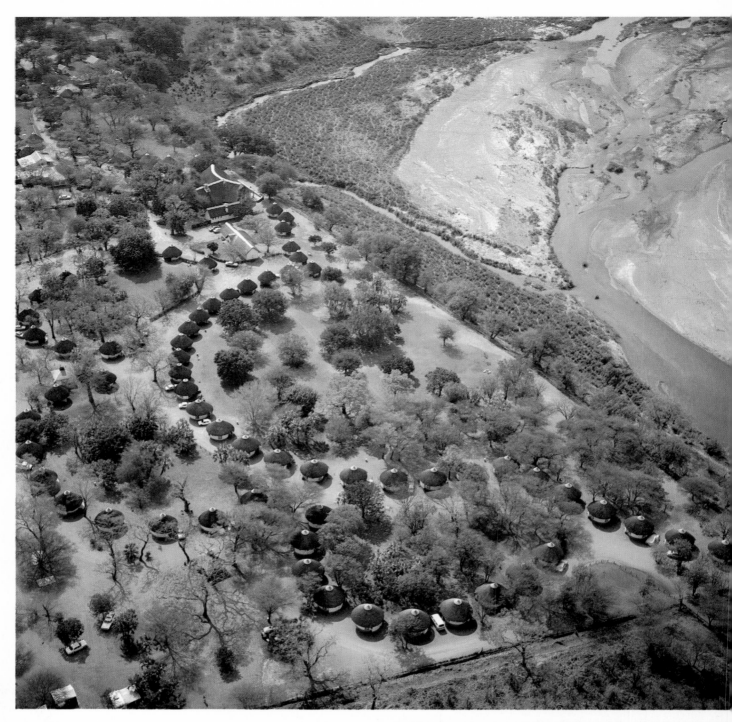

Camp life. An aerial view of Letaba (1), in the central region of the Kruger National Park, at the strategic junction of the three major roads and well placed above a sweeping bend in the Great Letaba River. Elephant, buffalo, zebra, hippo, crocodile and many species of antelope can all be viewed from the comfort of the camp's pleasant terraces. Letaba's rondavels (2) are unpretentious, comfortable and equipped with the essentials for cooking and eating, though there is a central restaurant.

4

5

7

Skukuza is the largest camp in the Kruger National Park and here elaborate displays (3) educate visitors in the ways of the wild.

In the Sabie-Sand Private Nature Reserve, dinner in the *boma* (4) is a highlight of a stay at the Mala Mala Lodge, as is game viewing from an open Land Rover (5). But the private reserves also offer visitors the opportunity to 'rough it', and at Timbavati guests enjoy a bush breakfast (6) near Tanda Tula Lodge while hikers set out from the M'Bali tented camp (7) in Umbabat.

1

2

3

4

5

6

Giraffes (1) are among the more common sights in the southern parts of the Kruger National Park, the largest concentration being near the Satara and Crocodile Bridge camps. They have just one natural enemy: the lion. Despite their size (as much as six metres tall and weighing up to 1,5 tons), giraffes are masters of camouflage, blending well with their dappled surroundings.

The Kruger National Park's smaller fry include the tree squirrel (2) and lesser-masked weavers (3), arguably the most adept of all nest-builders. Among the park's many species of antelope are the waterbuck (4), with their shaggy grey coats and the telltale white circle around the rump, and the roan (5), one of the rarest species in the park. Crocodiles (6) are common in the park's rivers and are a constant threat to animals quenching their thirst.

The chacma baboon (1) is everywhere in the Kruger National Park; in fact it is common throughout the country. It is inquisitive, cunning, and not above stealing from visitors' cars.

The park has a population of some 25 000 buffalo (2 & 5) – a healthy figure, as eight decades ago the species almost became extinct when rinderpest devastated the herds. Outwardly placid, the buffalo is nevertheless one of the most dangerous of animals when wounded or molested. The big predators tend to leave them alone, but when a herd does come under threat it forms a defensive ring, very much like a laager.

The blue wildebeest (3) is also fairly abundant in the park, as is the whitebacked vulture (4), a voracious scavenger which is quick to arrive at the scene of death. This summer-nesting species lays a single egg, incubated by both parents.

2   5

3   4

1

2

3

5

Elephants are among the most endearing of all animals and are often responsible for halting traffic in the Kruger National Park as visitors jockey for photographs (1). Although old males tend to live alone, elephants are social animals and live in family units — a mother and her offspring — which may group together to form herds (2 & 3).

Because elephants have huge appetites and are generally destructive feeders — they will often push over fully grown trees to reach a few succulent shoots — they devastate the land, threatening not only the survival of other animals but themselves as well, unless their numbers are controlled. To this end annual censuses are taken and, where necessary, the animals are culled. This long-term management programme has stabilized the elephant population of the Kruger National Park at around 7 500, the majority living in the mopane-covered northern region. The mopane is a favourite food source and here (5) an adult strips a young shrub.

These gregarious giants of the veld are often near water as, like everything else about them, their daily intake is huge — about 130 litres for an adult. Family groups are commonly seen at the Kruger National Park's rivers, including the Letaba (4).

The park's elephants are notable for their unusually large tusks: over 20 bulls have been counted with one or both weighing more than 50 kg. One magnificent specimen, the late and lamented Mafunyane ('the irritable one'), had tusks as heavy as this, a prime prize for poachers.

1

2

3

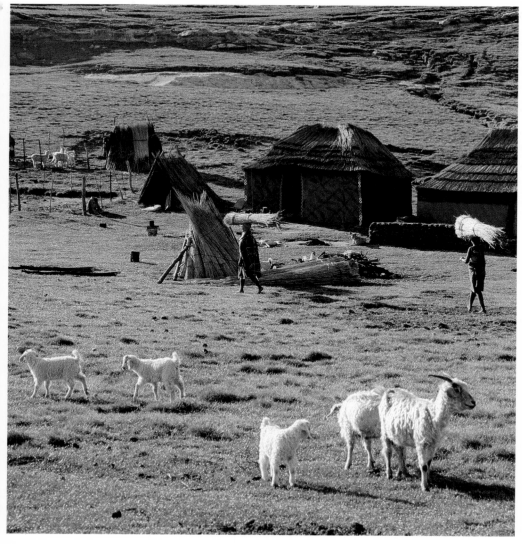

The Free State's plains tend to be bare, sparsely populated, undulating prairie land, epitomized by the lonely road between Ficksburg and Fouriesburg (1). It is the breadbasket of the country, with some 30 000 farms given over to wheat and maize as well as sheep and cattle. Livestock auctions, such as this one at Heilbron (2), are important events in the farming calendar. Water is scarce, and underground sources lifted from below by windmills (3) are often the principal supply rather than the supplementary.

Bethlehem (4), with the sandstone foothills of the Maluti Mountains in the distance, is typical of the Orange Free State's country towns: neat collections of unpretentious bungalows huddled around main street and Dutch Reformed church, surrounded by the dun vastness of a treeless land. When it does rain, the veld greens quickly, as it has done around this Sotho kraal in the Rooiberg range (5).

Bloemfontein, the Orange Free State's only city and the Republic's judicial capital, was founded in 1846, when the Great Trek was eight years old and thousands of Cape settlers had crossed the Orange River in search of a new country. The seat of government was the Old Raadsaal (3), a modest building but palatial compared to the *hartbeeshuis* (2) in the grounds of the Old Presidency. This rude dwelling is a reconstruction of the home of the Brits family, on whose farm the capital was built.

A good view (5) of the central city with its contemporary and mostly uninspired architecture is gained from the top of nearby Naval Hill. There are, however, several imposing buildings of more elegant proportions such as the Afrikaans Literature Museum (1).

Despite its agricultural emphasis, the Free State has its share of heavy industry. The Sasolburg oil-from-coal plant (4), for example, was built by the South African Oil and Gas Corporation, in the 1960s, on a huge coalfield just south of the Vaal River. Of slightly earlier vintage are the vast goldfields around the town of Welkom, which was established in 1947 and now has a population of 150 000. Such operations are not necessarily detrimental to Nature in every respect: this pan (the water is pumped from the mines) provides a fine feeding ground for a flock of flamingoes (6).

5

6

The Golden Gate Highlands National Park, one of South Africa's 14 national parks, is an almost 5 000-hectare tract of rugged sandstone uplands in the Orange Free State, 360 kilometres south of Johannesburg. Famed for the shapes and colours (much is indeed golden) of its stark, hauntingly beautiful sandstone formations such as the Brandwag Rock (1) and the Mushroom

Rocks (3), the park also offers a splendid variety of bright wild flowers (fire and arum lilies, red hot pokers, watsonias), and of birdlife (the raptors, including the rare lammergeyer, are especially noteworthy), and is a paradise for climbers, riders and walkers, the two-day Rhebuck Trail (2) being particularly popular.

The park is also home to the black wildebeest (4), easily identified by its white tail. In fact the species is also known as the white-tailed gnu – gnu being a corruption of a Hottentot word which imitates the whistling sound the animal makes when alarmed.

Brandwag Lodge (5) offers sophistication in a rural setting: a fine restaurant and cocktail bar, luxury double and single rooms, as well as fully equipped family chalets.

South Africa's largest river, and principal source of water in a generally dry land, is the Orange, which rises high in the Drakensberg and rolls its way westward for 2 000 kilometres to the Atlantic Ocean, bringing sustenance to the otherwise arid northern regions of the Karoo, Bushmanland and the north-western Cape. Principal reservoir of the river's water is the 374 square-kilometre Hendrik Verwoerd Dam, which irrigates extensive areas of the Free State and, by means of two tunnels running southwards (one of 89 km, the other of 52 km), supplies much-needed replenishment to the Fish and Sundays rivers. The dam's resort (6) is a popular holiday venue.

Mountains of the dragon. The Great Escarpment reaches its most dramatic heights in the east, where the towering faces of the Natal Drakensberg rise, sometimes almost sheer, 3 000 and more metres from the plains of the Natal midlands. One access is via the foothills in the Witsieshoek region (2) bordering the Orange Free State and the tiny national state of Qwa Qwa. The Tugela River rises near Mont-aux-

Sources – at 3 282 metres, the highest of the Natal peaks – and after finding its way through the upper slopes (3) plunges 600 metres down the escarpment, through the magnificent Royal Natal National Park, with the ramparts of the Amphitheatre as its backdrop (1), and then meanders through 250 kilometres of often desiccated countryside to the eastern seaboard.

The Amphitheatre's Eastern Buttress, with its attendant Devil's Tooth **(4)**, is just one of the countless climbing challenges that draw mountaineers from all over the country, indeed the world. The Natal Parks are renowned for their comfortable but unobtrusive accommodation, and Tendele Camp **(5)** is no exception.

1

South of the Royal Natal National Park are two heights of special splendour: Mnweni, or 'place of fingers', but commonly known as the Rockeries (3 116 metres) and, farther on, an eastward-projecting ridge of lofty peaks: Cathedral; Bell; Outer Horn; Inner Horn, and smaller ones known as the Mitre and the Chessmen. Views everywhere are spectacular, none more so than through the Map of Africa (1) and up the winter-browned slopes of the 'Little Berg' towards Cathedral peak (4).

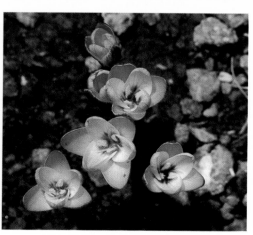

But in the 'Berg, beauty lies not only in the grand panorama: everywhere wild flowers delight the eye: *Helichrysum* spp. (2 & 3); *Hesperantha* spp. (5 & 7) and the delicate cream and yellow *Protea subvestita* (6).

At the foot of the Natal Drakensberg lies the 35 000-hectare Giant's Castle Game Reserve, a natural paradise of grassy slopes and deep river valleys presided over by the basalt massifs of Champagne Castle, the Trojan Wall, eNjesuthi and, most majestic of all, the 3 314-metre high Giant's Castle itself, standing in stark whiteness above the Bushman's River (5). The reserve is home to a number of antelope species, including the stately eland (1) as well as smaller denizens such as the common girdled lizard (2) and common night adder (3). The Giant's Castle rest camp, in a setting of wild flowers, is especially attractive, and there are mountain huts for hikers, climbers, riders, trout fishermen and bird watchers. Lone Basotho horsemen (4) are not an uncommon sight in the high mountain passes.

1

2

3

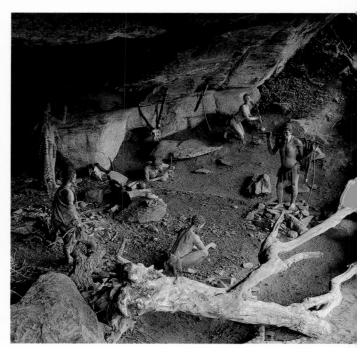

4

The deep pink flowerhead of *Watsonia meriana* **(1)**, a welcome splash of colour high in the 'Berg where the Sani Pass **(2)** makes its tortuous way up the escarpment. The pass, one of a few linking Natal with the land-locked mountain kingdom of Lesotho, is the highest in southern Africa, some 2 900 m above sea level at its summit.
Bushmen once hunted and gathered food in the foothills of the Drakensberg and made their

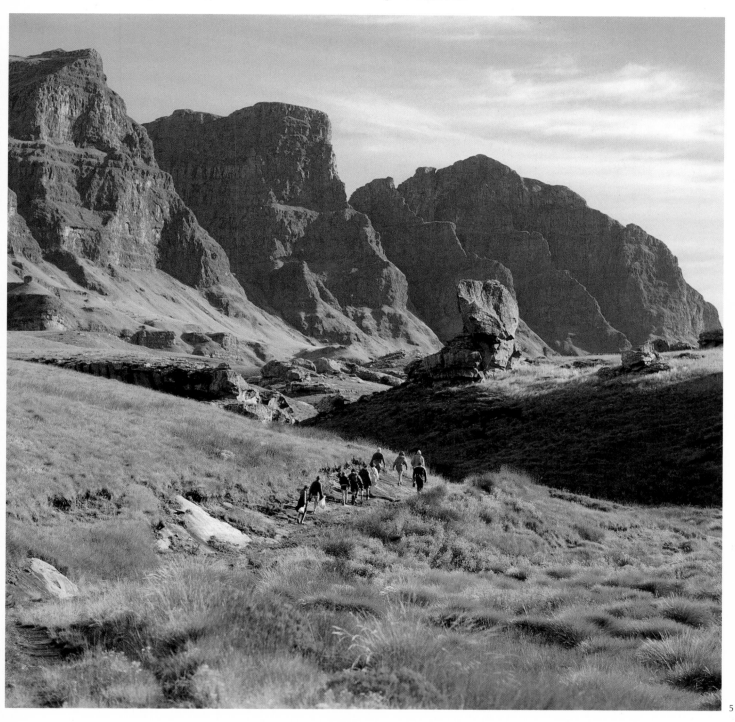

5

homes in the many shallow caves and rock shelters at the base of sandstone cliffs. They are long gone, but their art, one of the land's greatest treasures, remains. The smooth surface of the rock gave them an ideal 'canvas' for its expression and the hunting scene depicted here **(3)** is part of one of the many galleries to be seen throughout the Natal Drakensberg. In the Main Caves, at Giant's Castle, is a reconstruction of how Bushmen lived in their shelters **(4)**.

   The towering crags are a constant challenge to rock climbers but, for the less adventurous, the grassy lower slopes are criss-crossed with tracks to be explored **(5)**.

The Zulu people number between six and seven million, and are the largest of southern Africa's ethnic groupings. Their 'homeland' is KwaZulu, a patchwork of territories scattered about Natal, self-governing but not yet fully independent: Chief Minister Mangosuthu Buthelezi and his government would prefer an integrated South African state in which power is shared rather than divided. Much of the land is over-grazed and poor, with erosion an ever-present threat. The 'beehive' huts (3) are quintessentially Zulu. Facilities for the large rural population are for the most part woefully inadequate – the river is often the only source for household water (1) and transport frequently an ox-drawn sledge (4).

The Zulus, most powerful and warlike of the 19th century black nations, have a proud history and strong cultural traditions, though many of the latter are being eroded by western industrial influences. The 'warrior' (2) is costumed for the tourist's benefit; but the young woman (5) is dressed in the distinctive manner sometimes still seen in the Ixopo region of southern Natal.

1

1

2

The daily round in KwaZulu. A woman makes a hide skirt (3) while others prepare reed bundles for thatching (1); children attend an open-air primary school (4) and a matron in more traditional dress visits the local store (5). Huts dot the rolling hills close to the Transkei border (2).

Natal's English heritage is evident everywhere but especially in the country areas where 'the club' and polo (2) are well supported; the colonial traditions are loyally, sometimes aggressively preserved.

Reminders of a troubled past are these relics of Anglo-Zulu conflict during the 1870s (3).

Although cattle are farmed extensively in the Natal midlands (4), sugar (1) has been one of Natal's economic mainstays since the first of thousands of indentured Indian labourers arrived in the 1860s.

The Howick Falls (5), on the Mgeni River before it winds through the Valley of a Thousand Hills, are among the country's loveliest.

1

2

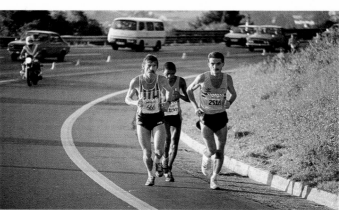

6

Pietermaritzburg (1), the capital of Natal, is a charming city, albeit a small one, nestled in the misty uplands some 90 kilometres inland from the coast. Colonial influences are strong here, too, and like Durban, 'Maritzburg has a substantial Indian community (2). Among the city's places of interest are the Botanic Gardens (4) which have a 46-metre high fig tree, a splendid avenue of planes and a great wealth of indigenous and exotic plantlife.

A modern dual-carriage highway now links Pietermaritzburg with Durban, but for those not in too much of a hurry to reach the beach, the old road, a narrow ribbon that wends its way up hill and down dale, provides an alternative route. The scenery is splendid, especially the Valley of a Thousand Hills (5). Most prominent of its features is Natal's Table Mountain, a flat-topped 658-metre high massif whose summit (easily reached from the western side) offers unrivalled views. The 'old road' is also the route of the annual Comrades Marathon, one of the most punishing of the world's ultra long-distance runs (6). Also worthy of attention and not too far off the motorway is the Mariannhill Monastery (3).

South Africa's playground. Durban is the country's largest port, third largest city, busy centre of industry and commerce, and paradise for pleasure-seekers – especially from the land-locked Transvaal, some seven hours' drive away. Its beachfront **(1-5)** is a three-kilometre strip of modern hotels, an aquarium, bowling greens, playgrounds, amusement parks, gardens, paddling pools, tearooms, some excellent restaurants, a mini-town (scale 1:24), fishing jetties, and magnificent golden beaches sloping steeply into the warm, roller-waved Indian Ocean.

4

5

6

7

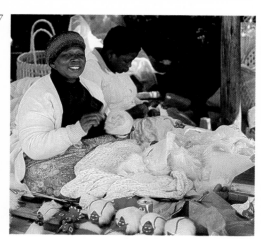

Tourism is Durban's most obvious industry and during the holiday seasons the city is invaded by up-country folk eager for the sea, a tan, and fun. The beachfront amusement centre (1 & 3) and the slides at Waterworld (2) provide plenty of the latter. While the city caters well to the masses there is an impressive range of luxury accommodation (4) for the more affluent. The rickshaws (5), each drawn by a Zulu in imposing regalia (the costume is an imaginative invention, not traditional garb) are as much part of the beachfront scene as candyfloss and icecream (6) and Zulu handicrafts (7).

Durban's harbour **(1-4)**. The bay is almost land-locked; the entrance narrow and, until the turn of the century, blocked to ocean-going ships by an unpredictably shifting sandbar. The harbour now handles over half the cargo passing through South Africa's ports. It is also home to the Royal Natal Yacht Club **(3)**.

The City Hall **(5)** dominates the central business district and, lending authority to its late-Victorian style is a statue to the old Queen **(8)** in an adjacent park. She would not have been amused by the punk fashions of these girls waiting for a bus **(6)**. The City Hall has an excellent library, art gallery, museum (housing, among other intriguing exhibits, the most complete skeleton in existence of the extinct dodo) and an auditorium seating 2 500 people. Adding a splash of colour to the city centre are the flower sellers **(7)** in front of the Post Office.

1

2

3   4

6

Eastern, Western and African cultures co-exist in Durban, giving the city a mix that is unique, vibrant and sometimes volatile. Glimpses of this milieu are: the Grey Street Mosque (1), the largest in the southern hemisphere (the tall white building in the background is the new beachfront Holiday Inn); a scene at the municipal market (2); a spice hall at the Oriental Bazaar (3); a Hindu wedding (4); golf at the Country Club (5); chess in Medwood Gardens (6); a Sunday afternoon boxing match (7); and an enthusiastic soccer crowd (8) at the stadium at Umlazi, one of Durban's satellite black townships.

1

2

3

Leaving Durban on the North Coast road the traveller passes a string of towns and attractive resorts, but within a few hours the scene changes dramatically as one enters the realm of Zululand's reserves – each remarkable for its beauty and wildlife. None is more so than St Lucia, a vast system of lakes, coastal forests and dunes. Not surprisingly, wildlife is prolific and the visitor is assured of good sightings of hippo, crocodiles, flamingoes and pelicans **(1)**. Among the many camps is picturesque Charter's Creek **(2)**, a complex of self-contained rondavels and cottages. Angling **(3)**, too, is excellent and fishermen are drawn to the area from all over the country, but it is Sodwana Bay **(5)** to the north of St Lucia that is arguably the mecca for South Africa's angling fraternity. Among the many smaller creatures found along the Zululand coast are fiddler crabs such as this specimen **(4)**.

Inland from the coast is the renowned Umfolozi Game Reserve which takes its name from the Black (**4**) and the White Umfolozi rivers. The name Umfolozi means 'zig-zag', an apt name for these two rivers which wander widely and then meet in this unspoilt land. Umfolozi is home not only to the world's largest concentration of white rhino but also to the black rhino (**6**).

Lions (1) also roam the reserve as does the stately nyala (3) which in Zululand reaches the southern limit of its distribution. Birdlife is prolific, and includes the hadeda ibis (2) which fills the morning and evening air with its raucous call. Insects form the bulk of the hadeda's diet, but a pyrgomorphid locust (5) is safe enough because of its foul taste.

Farther north, through a gap in the Lebombo mountains, lies the Mkuzi Game Reserve, as rich in the variety of its vegetation as in its animal life. Giant sycamore figs (2) are a feature of the park, as are its many watercourses and shallow sweetwater pans which sustain the reserve's inhabitants: cheetah (1), grey heron (3), African jacana (4), and the white rhino (5) to name but a few.

The white rhino once occurred widely in Africa, but with the expansion of 19th century settlement, the indiscriminate predations of sporting hunters and of superstitious poachers (quite erroneously, the rhino's horn is thought to have aphrodisiac properties) the numbers declined to the point where the species faced extinction. By the turn of the century there were just 30 specimens left, tucked into the 250 square-kilometre patch of Zululand territory between the two arms of the Umfolozi River. The tide of destruction was turned, however, with the creation of the Umfolozi Game Reserve. Official sanctuary saved the animals, and the numbers grew to such an extent that they began to pose a threat to their habitat. But with the development of immobilizing drugs and capture techniques, the Natal Parks Board started to 'export' the animals to depleted areas such as Mkuzi, the Kruger National Park and farther afield. By the 1980s well over 3 000 white rhino had found new homes.

Mkuzi's Msinga waterhole is one of two in the reserve where visitors can view game from a comfortable hide (3). The cool of early morning and late evening are the best viewing times and patience is rewarded as the animals come down to slake their thirst, among them kudu (1), warthogs (2) and zebra (4). Birds, too, are found in abundance at the waterholes, but for wetland birds few places can compete with the huge Nsumu Pan (5) at the confluence of the Mkuze and Umsunduzi rivers.

1

2

4

1

2

3

4

5

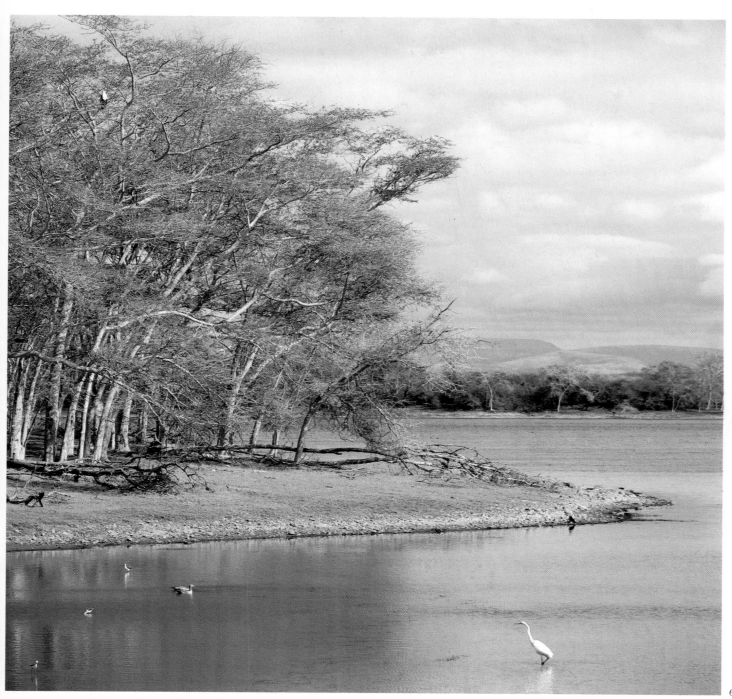

6

Ndumu (**1-6**) is the northernmost of the Zululand reserves, lying along South Africa's border with Mozambique nearly 500 kilometres from Durban. It is not a big reserve but what it lacks in size it makes up for in quality – Ndumu's 11 000-hectare floodplain is an intricate lattice of freshwater pans, such as Nyamithi (**6**) where no fewer than 393 bird species have been recorded, many of them tropical species which reach the southern limit of their ranges here. The goliath heron (**5**) is not one of the rarer species of Ndumu – it is fairly common in many wetland areas – but few can fail to be impressed by its sheer size; mature birds can grow to 1,4 metres and have a wingspan of about 1,2 metres. Not surprisingly, the reserve attracts 'birders' from far beyond the country's borders, but botanists, too, are well rewarded, for among the many plant species is *Encephalartos ferox* (**1**), a member of the ancient cycad family, living fossils which have inhabited the earth for over 200 million years. Comparative newcomers to the stage, but no less impressive, are the sycamore figs (**4**).

In sharp contrast to the pristine reserves of Zululand is the almost continuous string of resort towns along the coast south of Durban towards the Transkei border. Among them are Margate (**3 & 5**) and Ramsgate (**4**) where the holiday-maker has everything to hand: safe bathing from beaches protected by shark nets, good surf, good fishing (**1**), and countless places to eat. For those needing respite, however, a day drive to the Oribi Gorge area is a delightful interlude. Here the Umzimkulu River carves its way through rolling hills, providing some spectacular scenery such as the view from the towering 'Walls of Jericho' (**2**).

1

3

4

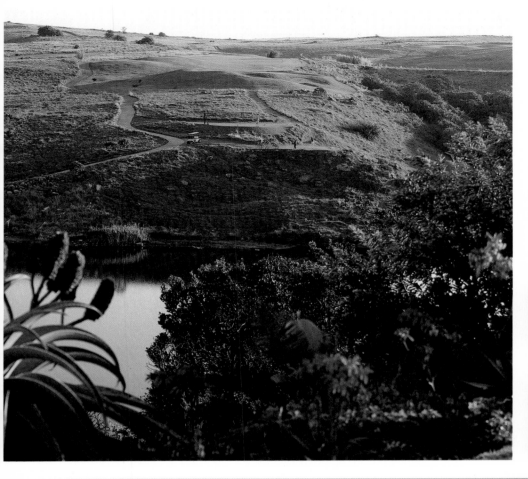

Just over the Transkei border is the Wild Coast Casino, a Sun City-type complex with a world-renowned golf course (**6**), Waterworld (**7**) and luxury hotel (**8**). Transkei, a national state, is poorly endowed with natural resources and relies heavily on tourism to balance its budget.

7

8

The Transkei is a poor country, its people mainly rural and eking a living from over-used land. From the main route through the Transkei, inland and via the capital of Umtata, branch a number of rough gravel roads leading to remote coastal villages, *en route* winding through rolling hills dotted with limewashed Xhosa homes (1), a region where people in traditional garb – older women often smoking their characteristically long pipes (2) – are a common sight. The undulating landscape ends abruptly at one of southern Africa's greatest scenic treasures, the Wild Coast, a challenge for

3

hikers (5) and a place for those who like their holidays to be simple and private. It is a lonely, strikingly beautiful shoreline of unspoilt beaches, estuaries and towering cliffs weathered into fantastic shapes such as Cathedral Rock (3), the Fallen Idol (4) and Waterfall Bluff (6) where one can walk between the rock face and the cascade plunging directly into the sea.

Quiet and restful, East London straddles the estuary of the Buffalo River in a narrow corridor of land sandwiched between the republics of Transkei to the east and Ciskei to the west. It is South Africa's only river port (1 & 2), handling outgoing citrus, mineral ores and wool as well as imports destined mainly for the Orange Free State. East London's immediate coastline comprises a string of sandy beaches – the Orient is said to be one of the safest in the country for bathers, while the Eastern (7) is more popular with surfers and anglers (4) – linked by rocky points with their intriguing inter-tidal pools (3). Even the business centre is relaxed, presided over by a stately city

1

2

3

hall, a monument to colonial forces who fell during the Anglo-Boer War (6) at its entrance.

Some 70 kilometres inland from East London is King William's Town, which had its beginning in 1835 as a garrison outpost built on the site of a mission station. Dressed stone is very much a feature of King William's Town's architecture – as indeed it is throughout the eastern Cape – and there are many fine, sturdy old buildings, including the Holy Trinity Church (5), built in 1856.

Grahamstown, its skyline dominated by the spire of the Cathedral of St Michael and St George **(1)**, is the heart of English-speaking South Africa. For it was to this region, the scene of many bloody frontier wars, that some 4 000 British immigrants were brought to settle and thereby provide a 'buffer' between the Cape Colony and the Xhosa-speaking tribes to the east. The statue (2) is part of the 1820 Settlers' National Monument which stands atop Gunfire Hill overlooking the city. Grahamstown started life in the early 19th century as a garrison, and faced its first great challenge in April 1819 when close on 10 000 Xhosa warriors descended on the outpost. It survived this and other crises, and over the years assumed its more peaceful Victorian character, a character which persists to this day (3). For obvious reasons Grahamstown is known as the Settler City, but it is also called the City of Saints – there are over 40 churches – and the City of Schools for its many places of learning, including Rhodes University (4).

The scattering of small towns and villages around Grahamstown are also redolent with their English heritage, none more so than Bathurst, complete with its 'Pig 'n Whistle' pub (5). The road from the village leads to Port Alfred on the Kowie River (7), a quiet, pleasant coastal resort, renowned for its lovely shoreline, especially popular with shell collectors: more than 1 800 shell species have been found in the area.

Typical of the eastern Cape landscape is this scene (6): gently rolling hills with lonely roads 'switchbacking' along their contours.

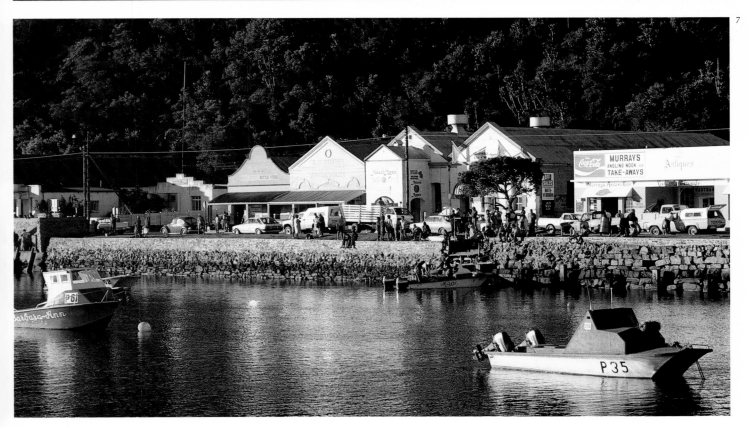

Port Elizabeth has a history dating back to 1799, when the new British regime built Fort Frederick on the slopes overlooking Algoa Bay, then at the extremity of the Cape Colony's frontier. It was here on the shores of the Bay that the 1820 Settlers made their lonely landfall. Today the city, capital of the eastern Cape, is one of the major industrial centres of South Africa and boasts the country's third largest harbour (3 & 4). Despite the focus on industry, however, Port Elizabeth is a pleasant, friendly place with much to offer the visitor: safe bathing beaches,

1

2

3

4

6

fine buildings – the elegant Public Library **(2)** and the terrace of Victorian Settler homes **(5)** being but two examples – and a snake park which houses over a thousand reptiles **(1)** (demonstrations and lectures are given daily). Next door is a museum and an oceanarium.

Undoubtedly a highlight of any visit to Port Elizabeth is a day trip to the Addo Elephant National Park **(6)**, haven for the last of the once-great Cape herds. It was here, in the early years of the century, that the unequal contest between farmer and wild animal was finally resolved. The survivors – not many more than ten elephants – fled to the impenetrable 'hunter's hell' region between the Zuurberg and the Sundays River valley – a rugged area but an ideal new home: today, the park's elephant population is three times denser than anywhere else in Africa.

South-westwards from Port Elizabeth, St Francis Bay sweeps in a gentle arc – a hundred kilometres of smooth sandy beaches, resorts, holiday cottages such as this one **(7)**, and a sea tailor-made for surfers and fishermen. Also to the west of Port Elizabeth the national road passes through verdant farmlands near Humansdorp **(8)**, gateway to the Garden Route.

1

2

3

4

5

The Cape's Garden Route, 230 kilometres from Storms River to Mossel Bay in the west, is one of the loveliest coastal strips in the world. Here there are beaches and bays, imposing cliffs, mountains, and everywhere the deep green of forest. What French explorer le Vaillant wrote of the area in the 1780s is apt today: 'The land bears the name Outeniqua, which in the Hottentot tongue means "a man laden with honey". The flowers grow there in their millions, the mixture of pleasant scents which arises from them, their colour, their variety, the pure and fresh air which one breathes there, all make one stop and think nature has made an enchanted abode of this beautiful place.'

Capturing some of the magic of the area are: *Erica chloroloma* (**1**); a giant yellowwood tree (**2**) in the Grootrivier Pass; the Knysna loerie (**3**), seldom seen but its loud, booming cry fills the forest; the vivid bracket fungus *Pycnoporus cinnabarinus* (**4**); a dew-laden spider's web (**5**); the ubiquitous rock hyrax (**6**); Nature's Valley lagoon (**7**); setting up camp in the Tsitsikamma Coastal National Park (**8**); and a baboon perched at the crown of a tall *Strelitzia* tree (**9**).

Within little more than a decade Plettenberg Bay has grown from a sleepy village to a bustling town packed to capacity during the summer season with holiday-makers from the coastal cities as well as upcountry. Eating places abound (2) and there is Beacon Isle, a hotel and time-sharing complex (1) perched on a rocky promontory in the bay. But for those who enjoy simpler pursuits, 'Plett', with its magnificent sweep of sandy beach and the lagoon of the Bietou River (3), offers superb angling, safe bathing and surfing — the bay is sheltered from the south by the Robberg, a high red-sandstone peninsula.

Thirty kilometres along the coast west of Plettenberg Bay is the pretty town of Knysna, lying on the shores of a vast lagoon and inland surrounded by dense brooding forests and fertile farmland (7). In an area famous for its natural beauty the sandstone heads (1), which guard the narrow access to the lagoon, are a highlight, while the lagoon (3 & 4) is itself a paradise for fishermen, divers, boating enthusiasts and windsurfers. Marine scientists also take a great interest in the lagoon, for it is an important nursery for a number of fish species and is also home to a rare sea horse.

The history of Knysna cannot be told without reference to George Rex who played a central role in the development of the town. Rex, an eccentric early 19th century English settler, lived in the area in grandly aristocratic, almost regal style, leaving behind a large family and a wealth of legend. His grave (2) lies on his farm Melkhoutkraal.

Between Knysna and the Wilderness lies another, even more extensive system of lakes and lagoons which provide sanctuary for birdlife such as the greater flamingo (5) as well as holiday playgrounds such as Pine Lake Marina (6) on the shores of Swartvlei.

The delicate pansy shell (8) is in fact not a shell but the exoskeleton of a sand-dwelling animal. Although synonymous with the Garden Route coast, it is found in estuarine conditions from Cape Infanta at the mouth of the Breede River to Durban.

The Garden Route continues: Swartvlei's outlet to the sea near Sedgefield (1); a stream stained dark by rotting vegetation meanders through indigenous forest (2); sheltered Herold's Bay with its cluster of holiday homes (3); and great loops of golden beaches (4 & 5).

West of Sedgefield and the Wilderness is the town of George, the imposing Dutch Reformed Church (6) serving its largely Afrikaans-speaking community. (Ironically the town was the first to be established by the British in South Africa.) The town is also the centre of a thriving furniture industry (7) which makes good use of local hardwoods.

6

7

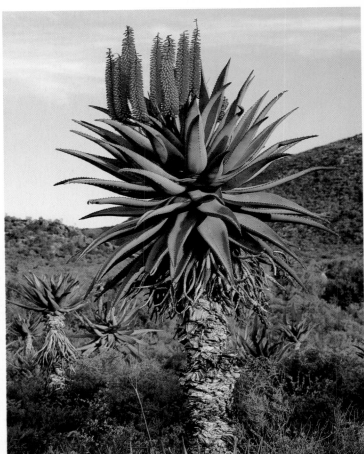

The road north from George to Oudtshoorn climbs in spectacular fashion over the Outeniqua Mountains, which rise 1 580 metres to George Peak. This is the dividing line between the narrow coastal zone and the Little Karoo, a barrier that proved nightmarish for the road engineers of the past. There are four major passes, including the Montagu (1), opened in 1847 and still in use. At its foot stands the old toll house (three-halfpence a wheel if you used a patent brake; 3d. a wheel if brakeless) and, half way up, there are the remains of the old and once much-needed blacksmith's repair shop.

The Little Karoo, a basin in the Cape Folded Mountain belt, is a strange world of imposing sandstone mountains, deep ravines, and a profusion of wild flowers including *Aloe ferox* with its fiery orange-red spikes (2). The soil, apparently arid in many places, is in fact very fertile, watered by the perennial streams of the Swartberg to the north and the Langeberg and Outeniqua ranges to the south, and by the Olifants River, which brings rich alluvial soil on its meandering way from the Great Karoo.

Oudtshoorn, principal town of the Little Karoo, was the world's ostrich feather capital, a thriving centre in the days prior to the First World War when plumes – those of the male bird (3) were most highly prized – adorned fashionable headgear. At one time the green lucerne fields of the area supported over 100 000 of the big birds; ostrich farmers made fortunes and built ornate 'feather palaces' (4). Although the ostrich boom is long past, there are still prosperous farms such as this one (5) at the foot of the snow-dusted Swartberg mountains. Feathers continue to be sold by public auction in the town.

One of southern Africa's most famous natural wonders is the complex of tortuous subterranean passages and chambers known as the Cango Caves. Hundreds of thousands of visitors make the journey each year to the Caves deep in the foothills of the Swartberg, and few fail to be awed by their fantastic dripstone formations (**1 & 2**). The Caves were 'discovered' in the late 1700s, but in

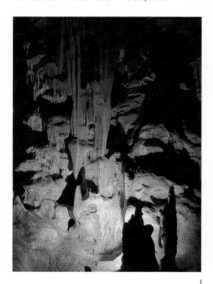

earlier times Bushmen made the entrances to these labyrinths their home, decorating the walls with their marvellous art. Largest of the chambers is the 107-metre-wide Grand Hall.

West of the Little Karoo is the Gamka River valley (**6**), between the Swartberg and Langeberg ranges, popularly known as 'The Hell'. The land is in fact fertile enough, though today only three families farm in this remote area, still laying out their figs (**5**) and other fruit to dry in the hot sun. The old water-driven flour mill (**7**), although no longer in use, is a reminder of a more active past.

Showing glimpses of the agricultural variety in the Little Karoo are this vineyard near Ladismith (**3**) and a farm in the Calitzdorp district (**4**).

4

5

6

7

The thirstlands. In geological terms the Great Karoo, a vast basin stretching from the highveld escarpment in the north to the Little Karoo in the south, is part of the Karoo System, an even more extensive area of deep sedimentary deposits that covers almost two thirds of the subcontinent. It is a country of far horizons interrupted by starkly sculptured dolorite rock formations such as the mountains near Sutherland (1); of blistering days, explosive sunsets and the clearest of nights, and, in springtime, of carpets of bright and hardy mesembryanthemums (2); and of dusty gravel roads plied by donkey-drawn carts (5). There are no perennial streams; flash-storms do more harm than good as the earth is tenuously protected by vegetation and vulnerable to erosion. Much of Laingsburg (6), one of the region's few towns and on the main north-south highway, was destroyed by sudden floods in 1981. But underground water sources are tapped by the ubiquitous wind-pump, sustaining the sheep farms. Sheep farming (3) is synonymous with the Karoo, home to most of southern Africa's 35 million sheep which browse the plains where huge herds of antelope, springbok, eland and hartebeest once roamed unhindered by fences and unmolested by the hunter's gun. There are wildlife sanctuaries, however, largest of which is the Karoo National Park (4) near Beaufort West.

1

The haunting Valley of Desolation (1), 14 kilometres west of Graaff-Reinet in the southern Karoo. The town (2) was capital of a rebellious, short-lived 'republic' in the 1790s, and much of its picturesque past has been preserved. Charming Victorian cottages (3) line the streets and many buildings have been meticulously restored – more than 200 are national monuments – including an entire street, Stretch's Court (4), now part of the Drostdy Hotel.

To the east of Graaff-Reinet, on the northern slopes of the Bankberg near Cradock, is the 6 536-hectare Mountain Zebra National Park (7), sanctuary to one of the world's rarest large mammals (5). There are also some fine examples of Bushman rock art in the area (6).

1

The 'Great North Road' near Three Sisters (2) where the national highway forks right to Bloemfontein and left to Kimberley via the towns of Strydenburg and Hopetown. Strydenburg (3) is a typical, tidy little centre of Karoo farming industry whose Afrikaans name translates into 'town of strife', commemorating an acrimonious local quarrel – over what to call the place! The area is one of the last outposts of the steam engine and enthusiasts are likely to be rewarded with the sight of one trailing its cloud of smoke across the veld (4).

2

It was close to Hopetown (1), south of Kimberley in the northern Karoo, that the first significant diamond find was made. In 1866 young Erasmus Jacobs, walking along the banks of the Orange, picked up a 21,25-carat stone (later named the 'Eureka'); three years later a second diamond, the 83-carat 'Star of South Africa' was found and eventually bought by the Earl of Dudley for £30 000. But the diggers who thronged the area found little else of value: the real wealth lay in the kimberlite pipes to the north. Hopetown today is the attractive headquarters of an agricultural region (cattle, sheep, fruit) enriched by the waters of the Orange.

In the far west of the Karoo, bordering the even drier Namaqualand region, is the Akkerendam Nature Reserve (5) in the Hantam mountains near Calvinia. Gemsbok, black wildebeest and the rare Hartmann's mountain zebra live here and each year the bleak landscape is transformed by the glory of carpets of wild spring flowers.

Diamonds, fabulous deposits of them, were discovered in 1870 in the 'yellow ground' of Colesburg Koppie in the wasteland north of the Orange River, provoking one of the 19th century's most frantic rushes. The koppie was literally torn apart, the 'blue ground' beneath found to contain even richer treasures, and the Big Hole (5) sunk ever deeper, with at times up to 30 000 men working its kimberlite claims. Around the now abandoned Hole grew the town of Kimberley, at first a chaotic collection of tents and shacks, canteens, doss-houses and dusty streets swarming with unkempt humanity; later, after the claims had been consolidated, it became an orderly and attractive town that has preserved much of its romantic past.

Diamonds are still mined in the area (1), and these, together with all other diamonds mined in South Africa and Namibia, are sorted at Kimberley's tall Harry Oppenheimer House, here forming the backdrop to the Digger Fountain (3) in the Oppenheimer Memorial Gardens.

A highlight of a visit to Kimberley is the 'living' museum where buildings and their interiors (2) have been re-constructed to capture something of the flavour of Old Kimberley. Reminders of the town's heyday are such homes as Melrose House (4) and the Kimberley Club (6), still very much in use and where Cecil Rhodes dreamed of empires.

Far to the south-west of Kimberley is Prieska on the banks of the Orange River; the grim stone fort with koker-boom sentries (7) is a relic of the Anglo-Boer War.

5

6

7

1

2

Centrepiece of the Augrabies National Park, a 9 000-hectare wilderness area around the lower reaches of the Orange River near the Namibian border, is the Augrabies gorge **(1)**, a nine-kilometre long, deep granite cleft through which the river, during one short stretch, plunges 146 metres to a deep pool in a series of spectacular cataracts. The main fall and the subsidiary Bridal Veil fall **(3)** are some 93 metres high. At peak periods the volume of water over the main Augrabies cataract is more than

3

half that of the mighty Victoria Falls in flood, but is dramatically concentrated across a far narrower width. Best viewing is from the north bank of the river.

The Klipspringer Trail, a long but undemanding hike through the southern area of the park, is a great attraction. It takes its name from the medium-sized antelope **(2)** whose sure-footedness makes it ideally adapted to the rocky terrain. In the dry scrubland of the region, the tall kokerboom **(4)** stands out, often adorned with the straggly 'condominium' nests of sociable weavers.

4

Some 250 kilometres north of Augrabies, in the great, infinitely remote tract of red duneland (2) is the Kalahari Gemsbok National Park which has a boundary, unrestricted by fences, with an even larger reserve in Botswana. Nearly a million hectares in extent, much of the national park is a virtually inaccessible wasteland of aeolian sand supporting hardy shrubs and scatterings of acacia (3).

But the aridity is deceptive, especially towards the western parts where the Auob River flows (albeit very seldom) and there is hidden water sustaining a varied wildlife. For example, in the Kalahari Gemsbok National Park more than 200 species of bird have been identified, including the white-backed vulture (1) often seen in large groups, hissing and squealing as they squabble over a carcass.

The ground squirrel **(4)** is constantly on the alert for predators, especially eagles, snakes and jackals. To protect itself from the intense Kalahari sun this rodent curls its bushy tail up over its head to form a parasol, but if the heat becomes too intense it takes refuge in the cool depths of its burrow.

The red hartebeest **(5)** was once in danger of becoming extinct because of wanton hunting, but today is plentiful in the Park. When water is available this grazing antelope will drink regularly, but in times of scarcity it seems able to go for months without drinking.

The ancient and mostly waterless 'rivers' of the Kalahari Gemsbok National Park, the Auob and, forming the eastern border with Botswana, the Nossob (which flows perhaps once every ten or so years) are the underground sources that nurture much of the reserve's prolific game population. Visitors might spot leopard (**1**) if they are lucky; will almost certainly see the black-backed jackal (**2**), springbok (**4**), bat-eared fox (**5**) and the striking gemsbok (**3**), which lends its name to the park. The antelope's magnificent long, sharp horns are formidable weapons of defence and are used to good effect against foes – there are accounts of even lions being bested by gemsbok.

The gemsbok also has a unique defence against another enemy – the heat. In the desert where there is little shade the danger of an animal's blood overheating and causing brain damage is ever present. The gemsbok, however, has a fine network of vessels in the nose through which blood passes *en route* to the brain. As it moves through this 'radiator' it is cooled by air inhaled through the gemsbok's nose.

Springtime in Namaqualand. One of only two true desert regions in South Africa, the wide strip of terraced sandveld leading up the west coast to the desolate lower reaches of the Orange River comes alive with a myriad wild flowers from about mid-August to mid-October each year. First to make their appearance are the white daisies (*Dimorphotheca* spp.) and *Oxalis* in all their forms and colours. Light-purple wild cineraria, darker purple *Lachenalia* and the famed red and orange Namaqualand daisies (*Ursinia* spp.) follow later.

1

2

3

4

5

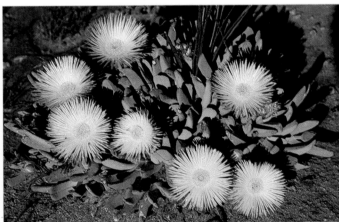

At the peak of the season, mid-September under ideal conditions, the visitor is rewarded with an unforgettable sight of multi-hued carpets of blooms stretching far to the horizon (2). Close-up, the individual flowers are just as lovely: *Gazania krebsiana* (1); *Ursinia* spp. (3), the classic Namaqualand daisy; *Drosanthemum hispidum* (4), a member of the great pan-tropical mesembryanthemum family which is centred in South Africa, where over 2 000 species have been recorded; and *Cheiridopsis marlothii* (5), found in hilly places.

The Namaqualand village of Steinkopf (1) was originally established for the Nama Hottentot community. The round 'matjie and sack' houses are designed for shelter from torrid sun rather than wind and rain, which are minimal. This is copper country: the Namas worked with metal long before the white man came; settler expeditions, one led by Commander Simon van der Stel himself, set out in the 1680s in search of the seams. The mines are still active: mills at Nababiep, Carolusberg and O'Kiep each handle over 2 000 tons of ore a day.

Far to the south of Steinkopf are the towns of Nieuwoudtville where, as with so many platteland towns, the Dutch Reformed Church **(3)** is the central feature, and Calvinia **(4)**, on the fringes of Namaqualand some 70 kilometres to the east. Calvinia, centre of South Africa's second largest wool-producing region after Harrismith in the Orange Free State, is an isolated little inland town set against the western edge of the Karoo and overlooked by the Hantam mountains.

The presence of spring flowers breaks the monotony of the harsh landscape **(2 & 5)** where drought is perennial and windmills tap underground water to sustain the farms.

The Cape's west coast is a region of harsh, lonely, beautiful stretches of rocky, sand-blown shorelines backed by raised beaches; of sparse and hardy vegetation, and of occasional exquisite little bays, some such as Lamberts Bay (2) and Doringbaai (3), providing safe anchorage for fishing fleets. Climate, the nature of the land and of the sea are influenced by the cold north-flowing Benguela current, which enriches the inshore Atlantic Ocean with nitrates and oxygen. Marine life thrives, sustaining both the country's fishing industry and seabirds — millions of them.

For the Cape cormorant (1) anything from scraps of vegetation to a frayed twist of nylon rope is acceptable in the making of its rude nest. Bird Island (4 & 5) is aptly named for here, as on many of the offshore islands along the West Coast, seabirds nest and roost in bewildering numbers. The gannet skypointing (6) does so to indicate non-aggressive intentions towards neighbouring birds.

4

5

6

1

2

3

The West Coast's Saldanha Bay **(2)** is one of the very few natural harbours along South Africa's entire shoreline: the first settlers, however, chose the more exposed Table Bay for its fresh water resources. Saldanha, though, is headquarters of a lively fishing and fish-processing industry, outlet for iron, manganese and other northern Cape mineral ores, and site of a naval training centre. A long narrow waterway extends southwards from Saldanha Bay, forming Langebaan Lagoon, a conservation area (now being developed as the Langebaan National Park) and playground for water sport enthusiasts **(3)**. Marcus Island **(1)** is part of the Park and home to colonies of jackass penguins, so-named for their call, which resembles the bray of a donkey. To the north of Saldanha lies a number of tiny fishing communities such as that of Paternoster **(5)** at Cape Columbine and the beautiful, unspoilt sweep of St Helena Bay **(4)**.

4

5

Inland from the southern West Coast, the landscape becomes gentler (1) with farmlands sprawling way into the distance – wheat, grapes and citrus are all grown on the fertile plains of the Olifants River valley. To the east of Clanwilliam in the north and Citrusdal in the south, however, the land rises abruptly into the Cedarberg. Although a few remote farms nestle in the more accessible valleys of the range and herds of

1

goats (2) may be seen in the higher terrain, the greater portion of the Cedarberg is a vast wilderness area some 71 000 hectares in extent. Entrance to the area is restricted, but for hikers and climbers it is well worth the minor inconvenience of obtaining a permit to spend time among the crags and peaks with their bizarre rock formations, cascading mountain streams, unique flora and magnificent views.

Slightly to the east of the reserve, but still very much part of the Cedarberg, is the picturesque village of Wuppertal (3 & 4), founded by the Rhenish mission in 1830 and named after a town in Germany. It is a surprising hive of activity in an otherwise quiet region, producing the *velskoen* (a rough hide shoe), processing tobacco, and sorting and packaging rooibos tea.

The haunting world of the Cedarberg where weird, eroded rock formations (2 & 4) dominate the skyline, dwarfing the intruder. Bushmen once took refuge among these krantzes and kloofs, but the only evidence of their presence is the remains of their subtle and sensitive art (1), reminding us here that many animals, too, are long gone from the region. Among the survivors are numerous reptile species such as *Pseudocordylus capensis,* the crag lizard, (3) which continue to soak up the sun as they have for aeons past.

In his campaign against elusive Boer guerilla commandos in the later stages of the Anglo-Boer War, Lord Kitchener erected 8 000 blockhouses such as this one (1) guarding a rail bridge near Wolseley. By contrast, Tulbagh (2-5), set in a peaceful valley at the foot of the Witsenberg range, charms the eye and rests the spirit. Founded in 1699, it began to assume its present, dignified character in the 1790s. Part of the town was destroyed by earthquake in 1969, but restoration work has repaired much of the damage done to its historic past: in Kerk Street alone, 32 lovely buildings, including the one shown (4), have been rebuilt and now form the largest concentration of national monuments in South Africa. Among the elegant gabled houses of Tulbagh are also Cape Dutch homes with simpler but no less pleasing lines (3). Some of the finest white wines in the country come from the Tulbagh valley, and at the Drostdy an old wine press stands sentinel (2), a reminder of times when wine making was less mechanized than it is today.

To the east of Tulbagh, in the mountains around the picturesque town of Ceres, the Breede River begins its long journey to the coast as a purling stream **(6)**. This is the heartland of the Cape Folded Mountains that extend in an irregular L-shape of twisted ranges from the Cedarberg in the north to the Tsitsikamma mountains in the east. The high peaks such as Mostertshoek **(7)** are regularly capped with snow in winter.

7

The south-western Cape is a land of mountains and valleys, few so spectacular as those of the Hex River area (1), its scenic richness well matched by the wealth of its vineyards – the area produces most of the table grapes exported from the country.

The rolling countryside at the foot of the mountains of the southern Cape is also lush farming land (2 & 4) characterized by great fields of wheat. Near to the town of Swellendam, which lies in the fertile valley of the Breede River beneath the peaks of the Langeberg, is the Bontebok National Park, a haven for a now substantial bontebok population (3). The species came close to extinction in the 1930s and was saved only by the timely action of a few concerned farmers who gave it sanctuary. The original park was started with a breeding stock of just 17, but poor grazing and other problems prevented success and the antelope only began to thrive when the park was transferred to its present site. Today there are more than 400. The park is also rich with other animals and birdlife is particularly prolific. Here a malachite sunbird (5) feeds from the common pincushion protea *Leucospermum cordifolium*.

2

3

5

4

The De Hoop Nature Reserve **(1)** near Bredasdorp is sanctuary for 1 400 plant species – most falling into the coastal fynbos classification and of which 25 are considered rare or endangered – and for a number of Cape mountain zebra **(6)**, also a threatened species. The reserve is the centre of a major controversy with a number of conservationists concerned about the effects of planned use of the area by the military.

The flower-strewn coastline east of the Cape Peninsula has wide sandy beaches, attractive embayments, small fishing communities, seaside towns and villages, as well as camps and caravan parks that draw Cape-tonian weekenders in their droves.

3

Among them are Gordon's Bay (2), tucked into the eastern corner of False Bay, Pringle Bay (4) near Cape Hangklip, and Hermanus (5), originally a fishing village, now a substantial residential and holiday centre, renowned within the angling fraternity. Picture (3) shows a ramshackle fisherman's cottage at Waenhuiskrans near Cape Agulhas, southernmost point of the African continent.

The extremely rare marsh rose (Orothamnus zeyheri) (7) is a member of the protea family and today is found only in Kogelberg Forest Reserve high above Betty's Bay and in the mountains above Hermanus.

4

6

5   7

The Cape winelands are famed not only for the wines they produce but for the exceptional beauty of their towns, villages and countryside. Stellenbosch, founded by Governor Simon van der Stel in 1679, is the oldest of the larger settlements and the second oldest town in South Africa. Age apart, however, many of its historical buildings, such as Krige's Cottages **(1)** and oak-lined vistas such as the one leading to the Dutch Reformed Church **(2)**, make Stellenbosch a tourist attraction in its own right. The town has great vitality, too, for it is the hub of the winelands and the seat of the University of Stellenbosch.

The gracious Lanzerac Hotel **(3)**, just outside Stellenbosch, is famed for its lunchtime spread and a popular stop-off for visitors to the town. The homestead at 'Meerlust' **(4)**, a prominent wine estate in the region, shows Cape Dutch architecture at its best and although it is not open to the public, many such as 'Simonsig' **(5 & 6)** are. These estates and other cellars are visited by hundreds of thousands of people each year, eager to see how wine is made and to sample the produce.

Franschhoek – 'French corner' in translation – takes its name from the hardy Huguenot pioneers, French refugees from the religious persecution of the 17th century's Counter-Reformation, who settled in the countryside north-east of the Cape Peninsula in 1688. Industrious, a few of them with some knowledge of wine-making, they were a welcome addition to the tiny and sometimes beleaguered communities. A Huguenot museum (2) and memorial (3) are prominent features of the town.

Franschhoek is at the head of the fertile Groot Drakenstein valley, hemmed in by the tall Drakenstein and Simonsberg mountains, and an important wine farming (1 & 4) and deciduous fruit growing area.

Paarl – the Pearl – is a lovely town of many whitewashed period buildings nestling in a broad valley (2) at the foot of great granite domes (3) which, often glistening in the sunlight, have given the town its name. The stately old Nederduits Gereformeerde Kerk (4) is but one of Paarl's noteworthy buildings.

1

Second only to Stellenbosch as a wine capital, Paarl is the headquarters of the KWV, a para-statal body which presides over the affairs of the wine industry. The KWV is also an important winery and distillery in its own right and holds tours to its cellars, where huge oaken barrels (1) can be seen.

Best known of the Cape's wineries is probably Nederburg (6 & 7), founded close to Paarl in 1792 and now producing many fine vintages of certified Superior quality. The Nederburg Auction – a heady affair of lunching, tasting, sociability and serious business – is held each autumn (5). It is run by Sotheby's and on offer are vintages from the country's leading cellars.

LEGEND

1. Uganda
2. Lake Albert
3. Lake Victoria
4. Lake George
5. Lake Edward
6. Murchison Falls National Park
7. Masindi
8. Butiaba
9. Kampala
10. Entebbe
11. Kenya
12. Nairobi
13. Mount Kilimanjaro
14. Amboseli National Park
15. Chyulu Hills
16. Tsavo National Park
17. Rwanda
18. Burundi
19. Tanzania
20. Ngorongoro Crater
21. Serengeti Plains
22. Mwanza
23. Democratic Republic of Congo
24. Bukavu
25. Rift Valley
26. Great Rift Valley
27. Western Rift Valley
28. Rwenzori Mountains
29. Lake Tanganyika

AFRICA

5

6

7

Close to two million people live in greater Cape Town, a city of beauty and contrast sprawling around the grandeur of Table Mountain and over the hills and shores of a Peninsula that accepted, if not welcomed, South Africa's first white settlers.

For much of the summer a strong south-easter blows across False and Table bays, gusting unnervingly through the streets of city and suburb; in winter it is wet – and windy. But when the weather is good it is perfect, and Capetonians go about their mostly gentle pursuits with a lightness of spirit that has something to do with the clarity of the air, the greenness of the hills, the history in the stones, with the fine calendar of arts and entertainment – and a lot to do with their own undemanding priorities and innate good taste.

1

3

Along the eastern flank of Table Mountain are: Rhodes Memorial (2) looking north across the Cape Flats, with its tea garden (1) and fallow deer (4) – the forests and footpaths round about are well trodden by the city's burgeoning jogger population (3); Groot Constantia (5), one of the earliest and certainly the most imposing of the early Cape Dutch homesteads. It began as the private residence of Simon van der Stel, the Cape's first Governor and a man of simple but refined tastes, who supervised its construction and extension with loving patience, incorporating, as one writer has put it, 'European ideas, Asian craftsmanship and African materials'. From the very first years the estate produced its own, splendid wine.

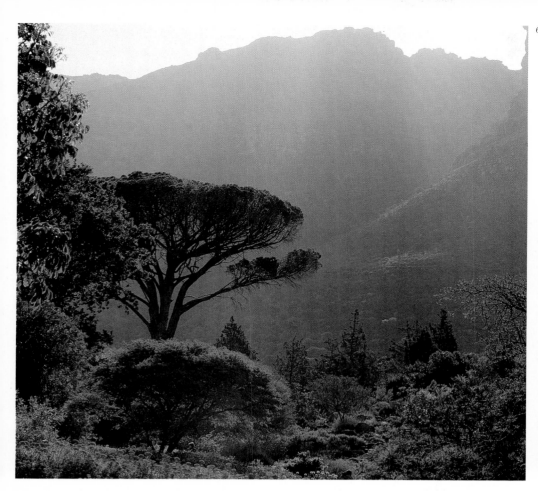

The botanic gardens at Kirstenbosch (6) where many exotic and indigenous plants are grown, including South Africa's national flower, the giant *Protea cynaroides* (7), and the University of Cape Town (8) which enjoys one of the grandest settings of any university anywhere in the world.

7

8

1

2

3

4

False Bay, so-named because early navigators returning from the east often mistook it for Table Bay, loops in a broad arc from Cape Point in the west to Cape Hangklip in the east. Its coastline is over 100 kilometres long, with the rapidly developing town of the Strand **(5)** at the base of its east-

ern arm. Across the bay, following the gentle sweep of white beaches interrupted by the odd rocky bluff, is Muizenberg of which Rudyard Kipling, who loved his summers at the Cape, wrote: 'White as the sands of Muizenberg, spun before the gale.' Indeed, it is only the regular blasting of summer winds that spoils the wide beach with its safe, warm surf. Nevertheless, the resort suburb, its beachfront dominated by the Pavilion **(4)** and other amusements, is a popular venue for beach lovers and any number of watersport competitions **(6)**.

Continuing the coastal drive from Muizenberg one passes through the pretty fishing harbour of Kalk Bay **(3)** – the naval base of Simonstown can be seen across the bay – and eventually reaches the Cape Point Nature Reserve **(1)** at the southern tip of the Peninsula. The reserve's wildlife includes bontebok, eland, mountain zebra and baboons **(2)** which can prove a hazard for hikers and picnickers (visitors are urged not to feed them).

Silvermine is another of the Peninsula's reserves, and vantage points here command dramatic views over the Cape Flats and beyond to the Hottentots Holland mountains **(7)**.

Returning from Cape Point along the western seaboard of the Peninsula the road clings tenuously to cliffs dropping sheer to the sea below. The winding route rates as one of the most spectacular scenic drives in the world and provides breathtaking views of places such as Noordhoek (1) with white sands stretching to distant Kommetjie; Hout Bay (4) with its picturesque, if sometimes noisome, fishing harbour (2); and Llandudno (3), an elite residential village surrounding a small secluded bay. Closer towards the city centre the air of tranquility changes abruptly as one reaches the built-up flatland of cosmopolitan Sea Point (6, 7 & 8) and, nearby, the famed beaches of Clifton (5).

4

6

7

8

Cape Town's old Lutheran Church (3) in Strand Street is one of the city's more dignified landmarks. It was built in 1774 as a storeroom by one Martin Melck, a devout Lutheran tradesman determined to circumvent a prohibition on places of worship other than Dutch Reformed.

Long Street was, until quite recently, the vibrant scene of the seamier kind of sociability. Now quieter, with much of its earlier architecture gone, there is still a hint of its past in one of the few remaining Victorian façades (1).

The South African Cultural Museum (2) adjoining the Gardens at the head of Adderley Street was the Old Supreme Court which was restored in the 1960s to house a number of important collections. The original building on the site was the slave lodge of the Dutch East India Company.

The Herbert Baker-designed Houses of Parliament (4) also number among the many splendid buildings that grace the bounds of Cape Town's Gardens – charming heir to Van Riebeeck's prosaic vegetable patch and internation-

ally famed for the wealth of its exotic trees, shrubs and flowers. Feeding the grey squirrels in the Gardens is a favourite pastime for youngsters (5); these engaging little animals are not indigenous to the country – they were introduced by Cecil John Rhodes. The Gardens Synagogue (8) is flanked by handsome oaks, some dating back to the time of the Cape's first Governor.

Once waves broke at the massive ramparts of the five-bastioned Castle of Good Hope (6) built between 1666 and 1679. Extensive reclamation has since pushed the ocean far back and the crash of surf has given way to the rumble of trains.

The Malay Quarter, or *Bokaap*, (7), where many of the city's Moslems live, is a dense huddle of cottages, some of them charmingly restored.

Cape Town's City Hall (1) has been replaced as the capital's administrative centre by the new Civic Centre, but not in the affections of Capetonians: some fine symphony concerts are performed in its massively-chandeliered auditorium. The grand Edwardian building overlooks the Grand Parade (2, 3 & 4), mid-week and Saturday meeting place where anything from a bunch of freshly cut flowers to a bolt of material can be purchased.

Open air markets are very much part of the city's street scene, and much favoured among locals and visitors alike is the one in cobble-stoned Greenmarket Square (5 & 7).

Cape Town's streets belong to the people and even in Adderley Street (8), the city's main thoroughfare, pedestrians rule the roads, paying scant attention to motor vehicles and traffic lights. Adderley Street, too, is a place for parades — everything from the sedate opening of Parliament cavalcade to the varsity rag procession. Here (6) are participants in the annual Cape Town Festival. The street, once part of the grand Heerengracht thoroughfare, was named after Charles Adderley, a 19th century British politician who fought hard and successfully to prevent the settlement of convicts at the Cape.

Today, Cape Town's dockland (**1 & 3**) shows only a glimmer of its former glory. In its heyday, Southampton-based Union Castle liners were given brass-band welcomes; ships steaming under a score and more flags queued to offload. But Cape Town is now remote from the trade and tourist routes (visits from liners such as *Queen Elizabeth II* are few and far between) and other harbours – in particular Durban and brand-new Richards Bay – are closer to the northern mines and markets. The port works to about a third of its capacity. Separating the waterfront from the old city is a forest of concrete towers (**2**) that would be at home in any modern metropolis in the world. Most have been built on land reclaimed from the sea and form part of a soulless business district known as the Foreshore.

Modern, but nevertheless part of the city proper, is the smokey-glassed façade of the Cape Sun Hotel (**4**).

In keeping with the trend elsewhere in South Africa, Cape Town has its fair share of covered shopping malls (**5 & 6**) which add a new brand of vibrancy to city and suburb.

4

5

6

Over a thousand metres high, monolithic, misty, moody, ever-changing with wind and season, Table Mountain (5) dominates the horizon, captivates the Capetonian heart. The mountain offers breathtaking views of city and sea from its summit, reached either by walking (3) (some paths are undemanding, others are extremely strenuous), climbing or by cable car (1).

Table Mountain has been proclaimed a National Monument and a sanctuary for its, in some cases unique, flora and fauna. Among the thousands of species are *Psoralea pinnata* (2); *Leucospermum cordifolium* (a member of the protea family) with a Cape sugarbird perched on its flowerhead (4); *Polygala bracteolata* (6); and *Helipterim speciosissimum* (7).

Republic of South Africa

Copyright by Rand McNally & Company, R.L. 75.1-5

Meters	Feet
6000	19685
4000	13124
3000	9843
2000	6562
1000	3281
500	1640
200	656
0	0

Kilometers   0   100   200   300   Km.

Statute Miles   0   100   200   300   Mi.

Scale 1:6,000,000

One centimeter represents 60 kilometers.
One inch represents approximately 95 miles.

INDIAN

OCEAN

INDEX